Dear Reader:

For more than 60 years, the image of the American flag being raised on Mount Suribachi has stood as an indelible symbol of heroism and victory, not only for the "greatest generation," but for the generations that followed. Yet, until the publication of James Bradley's remarkable book about his father and his comrades in arms, the story of the men at the base of that flag and the terrible battle they fought leading to that iconic moment has been virtually unknown, save to a very few.

I was proud to have the opportunity to bring James Bradley's book to the screen and to join him in honoring the memories of those men. I feel this story not only pays tribute to the men who raised the flag, but to so many anonymous heroes who bravely fought and died on Iwo Jima and a thousand other battlefields in World War II

Sincerely,
Clint Eastwood

FLAGS
OF OUR
FATHERS

HEROES OF IWO JIMA

JAMES BRADLEY

with Ron Powers
adapted for young people by Michael French

Published by Laurel-Leaf
an imprint of Random House Children's Books
a division of Random House, Inc.
New York

Text copyright © 2001 by James Bradley and Ron Powers
Letter copyright © 2006 by Clint Eastwood

Originally published in hardcover in the United States by Delacorte Press, New York, in 2001. This edition published by arrangement with Delacorte Press.

Laurel-Leaf and colophon are registered trademarks of Random House, Inc.

www.randomhouse.com/teens

Educators and librarians, for a variety of teaching tools, visit us at
www.randomhouse.com/teachers

RL: 6.5

ISBN-13: 978-0-440-22920-9
ISBN-10: 0-440-22920-0

April 2005

Printed in the United States of America

10 9 8 7 6

Dedicated to the memory of
Belle Block, Kathryn Bradley, Irene Gagnon,
Nancy Hayes, Goldie Price, Martha Strank,
and all mothers who sent their boys to war

Listen to me, and follow my orders,
and I'll try to bring all of you
back safely to your mothers.

—SERGEANT MIKE STRANK

CONTENTS

ONE

Sacred Ground

*The only thing new in the world
is the history you don't know.*

—Harry Truman

In the spring of 1998 six boys called to me from half a century ago on a distant mountain, and I went there. For a few days I set aside my comfortable life—my business concerns, my life in Rye, New York—and made a pilgrimage to the other side of the world, to a tiny Japanese island in the Pacific Ocean called Iwo Jima.

There, waiting for me, was the mountain the boys had climbed in the midst of a terrible battle half a century earlier. The Japanese called the mountain Suribachi, and on its battle-scarred summit the boys raised an American flag to symbolize our country's conquest of that volcanic island, even though the fighting would rage for another month.

One of those flag raisers was my father.

The fate of the late twentieth and twenty-first centuries was

1

being forged in blood on the island of Iwo Jima and others like it in the Pacific, as well as in North Africa, parts of Asia, and virtually all of Europe. The global conflict known as World War II had mostly teenagers as its soldiers—kids who had come of age in cultures that resembled those of the nineteenth century.

My father and his five comrades—they were either teenagers or in their early twenties—typified these kids: tired, scared, determined, brave. Like hundreds of thousands of other young men from many countries, they were trying to do their patriotic duty and trying to survive.

But something unusual happened to these six: History turned all its focus, for 1/400th of a second, on them. It froze them in an elegant instant of one of the bloodiest battles of the twentieth century, if not in the history of warfare—froze them in a camera lens as they hoisted an American flag on a makeshift iron pole.

Their collective image became one of the most recognized and most reproduced in the history of photography. It gave them a kind of immortality—a faceless immortality. The flag raising on Iwo Jima became a symbol of the island, the mountain, the battle; of World War II; of the highest ideals of the nation; of valor itself. It became everything except the salvation of the boys who performed it.

For these six, history had a different, special destiny that no one could have predicted, least of all the flag raisers themselves.

My father, John Henry Bradley, returned home to small-town Wisconsin after the war. He shoved the mementos of his immortality into a few cardboard boxes and hid these in a closet. He married his childhood sweetheart. He opened a funeral home, fathered eight children, joined the PTA, the Lions, and the Elks—and shut out virtually any conversation on the topic of raising the flag on Iwo Jima.

When he died, in January 1994, in the town of his birth, he might have believed he was taking the story of his part in the flag raising with him to the grave, where he apparently felt it belonged. He had trained us, as children, to deflect the phone-call requests for media interviews that never diminished over the years. We were to tell the caller that our father was on a fishing trip, usually in Canada. But John Bradley never fished. No copy of the famous photograph hung in our house. When we did manage to extract from him a remark about the incident, his responses were short and simple, and he quickly changed the subject.

And this is how we Bradley children grew up: happily enough, deeply connected to our peaceful, tree-shaded town, but always with a sense of an unsolved mystery somewhere at the edges of the picture.

A middle child among the eight, I found the mystery tantalizing. I knew from an early age that my father had been some sort of hero. My third-grade schoolteacher said so; everybody said so. I hungered to know the heroic part of my dad. But try as I might, I could almost never get him to tell me about it.

John Bradley might have succeeded in taking his story to his grave had we not stumbled upon the cardboard boxes a few days after his death.

My mother and brothers Mark and Patrick were searching for my father's will in the apartment he had maintained as his private office. In a dark closet they discovered three heavy cardboard boxes. In those boxes my father had saved the many photos and documents that came his way as a flag raiser. All of us were surprised that he had saved anything at all.

Later I rummaged through the boxes. One letter caught my eye. The cancellation indicated it was mailed from Iwo Jima on February 26, 1945, written by my father to his folks just three days after the flag raising: "I'd give my left arm for a good shower and a clean shave, I have a 6 day beard. Haven't had any soap or water since I hit the beach. I never knew I could go without food, water or sleep for three days but I know now, it can be done."

And then, almost as an aside, he wrote: "You know all about our battle out here. I was with the victorious [Company E,] who reached the top of Mt. Suribachi first. I had a little to do with raising the American flag and it was the happiest moment of my life."

The "happiest moment" of his life? What a shock! If it made him so happy, why didn't he ever talk about it? Did something happen either on Iwo Jima or in the intervening years to cause his silence?

Over the next few weeks I found myself staring at the photo on my office wall, daydreaming. Who were those boys with their hands on that pole? Were they like my father? Had they known one another before that moment or were they strangers united by a common duty? Was the flag raising the "happiest moment" of each of their lives?

The quest to answer those questions consumed four years of my life and ended, symbolically, with my own pilgrimage to Iwo Jima.

· · ·

Iwo Jima is a very small place to have hosted such a savage battle. Only eight square miles, the tiny island barely crests the seemingly infinite Pacific. The value of capturing this speck of land for the Americans was its location and its two airfields. The island provided a place for American planes to stop and refuel on crucial bombing missions to and from Japan.

Not many Americans make it to Iwo Jima these days. It is a dry wasteland of black volcanic ash that reeks of sulfur (the name means "sulfur island"). A closed Japanese naval base, it is inaccessible to civilians except for rare government-sanctioned visits.

It was the commandant of the Marine Corps, General Charles Krulak, who made the trip possible for me, my seventy-four-year-old mother, three of my brothers—Steve, Mark, and Joe—and many military men and women. One of first things we did on the island was to walk across the beach closest to Mount Suribachi, on the black volcanic sands. On their invasion maps the Marines had dubbed it "Green Beach," and it was across this killing field that young John Bradley, a Navy corpsman, raced under heavy fire. I watched as my mother made her way across that same beach, sinking to her ankles in the soft volcanic sand with each step. "I don't know how anyone survived!" she exclaimed.

Then it was time for our family to ascend the 550-foot volcanic crater that was Mount Suribachi. My twenty-one-year-old father had made the climb on foot carrying bandages and medical supplies; our party was whisked up in vans. I stood at its summit in a whipping wind that helped dry my tears. This was exactly where that American flag was raised on a February afternoon fifty-three years before. The wind had whipped on that day as well.

From the edge of the extinct volcanic crater, we could view

the entire two-mile beach where the armada had discharged its boatloads of Marines. In February 1945 the Japanese could see it with equal clarity from the tunnels just beneath us. They waited patiently until the beach was crowded with American boys. They had spent many months positioning their gun sights. When the time came, they simply opened fire, beginning one of the great military slaughters of all history.

An oddly out-of-place feeling seized me: I was so glad to be there! The vista below us, despite the gory history, was invigorating. The sun and the wind seemed to bring all of us alive. At Suribachi you feel on top of the world, surrounded by ocean.

And then I realized that my high spirits were not so out of place at all. I was reliving something. I recalled the line from the letter my father wrote three days after the flag raising: "It was the happiest moment of my life."

We Bradleys then began to take pictures. We posed in various spots, including near the X that marks the spot of the actual raising. We had brought with us a plaque to personally commemorate the flag raising and our father's role in it. Joe gently placed the plaque in the dry soil.

IN MEMORY OF

JOHN H. BRADLEY

FLAG RAISER

2-23-45

FROM HIS FAMILY

I began to speak to the Marines who had gathered in front of our memorial.

I spoke first of the battle. It ground on over thirty-six days. It claimed 25,851 U.S. casualties, including nearly 7,000 dead. Most of the 22,000 defenders fought to their deaths.

It was America's most heroic battle. Two out of every three Americans who fought on this island were either killed or wounded. More medals for valor were awarded for action on Iwo Jima than in any battle in the history of the United States. To put that into perspective: The Marines were awarded eighty-four Medals of Honor in World War II. Over four years, that was twenty-two a year, about two a month. But in just one month of fighting on this island, they were awarded twenty-seven Medals of Honor, one-third of their accumulated total.

Next I showed the Marines the famous flag-raising photograph. I remarked that nearly everyone in the world recognizes it, but no one knows the boys.

I pointed to the figure in the middle of the image: solid, anchoring, with both hands clamped firmly on the rising pole. That's my father, I said. John Bradley was known to the other Marines in his company as "Doc," because he was a medical corpsman. He is the most identifiable of the six figures, the only one whose profile is visible.

I pointed next to a figure on the far side of John Bradley. Rene Gagnon, the handsome mill hand from New Hampshire, stood shoulder to shoulder with my dad in the photo, but he is mostly obscured by my father.

I gestured to the figure on the far right of the image, the leaning, thrusting soldier jamming the base of the pole into the hard Suribachi ground. His right shoulder is nearly level with his knee. His buttocks strain against his fatigues. This was Harlon Block, the athletic, independent-minded Texan. A star football player, he enlisted in the Marines along with all the seniors on his high school football team.

I pointed to the figure directly in back of my father: the boyish, freckle-faced Franklin Sousley, from Hilltop, Kentucky. He was fatherless at the age of nine and sailed for the Pacific on his nineteenth birthday.

Look closely at Franklin's hands, I asked the silent crowd in front of me. Do you see his right hand? Can you tell that the man in back of him has grasped Franklin's right hand and is helping Franklin push the heavy pole? The most boyish of the flag raisers, I said, is getting help from the most mature, Sergeant Mike Strank.

I pointed now to what can be seen of Mike. He is on the far side of Franklin. You can hardly see him. But his helping young Franklin was typical of him. He was respected as a great leader, a Marine's Marine. Finally I singled out the figure at the far left of the image—the figure stretching upward, his fingertips not quite reaching the pole. The Pima Indian from Arizona. Ira Hayes, I said. His hands couldn't quite grasp the pole.

Six boys. They form a representative picture of America in the thirties and forties: a mill worker from New England, a Kentucky tobacco farmer, a Pennsylvania coal miner's son, a Texan from the oil fields, a boy from Wisconsin's dairy land, and an Indian living on an Arizona reservation.

Only two of them walked off this island. A third was carried on a stretcher with shrapnel embedded in his side. Three were buried here.

Holy Land. Sacred ground.

TWO

All-American Boys

All wars are boyish, and are fought by boys.

—Herman Melville

I'm not a professional researcher, but I figured that if I could somehow dig deep enough, I might be able to learn something about these six boys, and especially about my silent father. I could not do this task alone. I would need other people, relatives and comrades of these six figures, to help me.

I began my research by buying a book about Iwo Jima and reading it. Then another. And another. I have since lost count.

I found names in those books—the names of the boys shoving that flagpole aloft.

Back in my office, I started to trace them. I phoned city halls and sheriff's offices in the towns where the flag raisers were born and asked for leads that would put me in touch with their relatives. I dialed the numbers, then waited through the rings for that first "Hello?" from a widow, sister, or brother of one of the boys whose hands had gripped the iron pole on Suribachi.

I widened my phone searches to include living veterans of Iwo Jima. I wanted their memories, too. Eventually I began to travel to the places where these people lived.

I wanted to know them as Marines, as fighting men who were also comrades. But I also wanted to know them as boys, ordinary kids before they became warriors.

What I found was that these six boys were very different from one another: the whooping young Texas cowboy; the watchful Indian; the happy-go-lucky Kentucky hillbilly; the serious Wisconsin small-towner; the handsome New Hampshire mill worker; the sturdy Czech immigrant.

And yet so similar.

They were nearly all poor. The Great Depression was a thread that ran through their lives. But then so did football, and religious faith, and strong mothers. So did younger siblings, and the responsibility of caring for them. And nearly all were described again and again as quiet, shy boys, yet boys whom people cared about.

John Bradley: Appleton, Wisconsin

My father was born in 1923 in Antigo, Wisconsin, the sturdy little town where he would return to raise his own family and where he would die. He attended St. John's Catholic School, where all eight of his own children would later enroll.

My dad's mother, Kathryn, the sister of a priest, was the religious worrier in the family; in fact, she was the worrier at large.

She worried about her children's future, she worried about money, she worried what the neighbors thought.

James J. Bradley, my dad's father, didn't worry about much at all. A veteran of the trenches in World War I, he was a hard-working railroad man, a laborer in a coal depot, a bartender. In Antigo James Bradley Sr. had proudly worn a railroad man's uniform and plied his skills in a variety of jobs on the freight trains that crisscrossed the state. His nickname was "Cabbage," given in good humor by his fellow workers at the rail yard for an accident involving spilled produce. Then the Depression cut deeply into rail freight, and layoffs crippled the livelihoods of James and many of his fellow "rails."

It was then that he uprooted his family for the more prosperous town of Appleton, population sixteen thousand, on the Fox River. In Appleton James Bradley struggled hard to rebuild his family's middle-class comforts. Ever the optimist, he produced five children—my dad, Jack, was the second eldest—and ever the pragmatist, he expected each one to help out with the household income. Jack and his elder brother, James junior, had newspaper routes throughout their childhoods. When they came home after making their collections each week, they often placed their money on the mantel. That money, perhaps along with the Blessed Mother, helped keep the family fed.

My father was a friendly boy with a ready smile, but he never said much. Talking drew attention, the last thing he wanted. Later, a severe case of acne deepened his pain at being observed.

He took refuge, with his pious mother, in the Catholic Church. It was there, from his vantage point as altar boy, murmuring the Mass prayers in Latin, that he started to notice— and admire—a particular category of businessmen: the funeral

II

directors of Appleton. These men, Jack thought, had a special way of walking up the aisle amid the incense smell at Mass or during a funeral service: confident, in control, but always accessible. Everybody seemed to know and respect them. The funeral directors were not merely men selling a commodity; other than clergy, they were the ones most intimately in touch with the townspeople in their times of sorrow and need.

Jack Bradley understood service. That was what an altar boy was, a "server." And now here were these models of service well into adulthood. By his early teens Jack Bradley was working part time at an Appleton funeral home. He was going to be one of these respected, dignified men of service.

Between World War I and World War II the town of Appleton, despite a deep and stubborn economic recession, had a certain optimism about it. For a kid especially, the rhythms of life were steady and reassuring. Tackle football in winter. Baseball in the spring. Swimming in Lake Park in the summer.

Betty Van Gorp, who eventually became Mrs. John Bradley, remembers a town of manicured lawns and clean streets. A town where people sat in swings or on the steps of their front porches on tree-shadowed summer evenings, listening to the cricket song swell up from the grass.

When my mother was in third grade she found a companion to walk her home from St. Mary's Catholic School: a new boy in town, a serious, quiet boy named Jack Bradley. Betty Van Gorp liked Jack Bradley, although she wasn't quite sure whether he liked her back. She appreciated the fact that Jack never cussed, even when it was so cold you wanted to scream at the weather. "Dad gum" was the worst that ever came out of his mouth.

It seemed an ideal life in an ideal town. But even ideal towns have their dangers and their sorrows, their abrupt reminders of the fragility of the human heart.

When Jack was ten years old a catastrophe struck of the sort his worrying mother could not have foreseen. Through a freak accident his five-year-old sister, Mary Ellen, came down with pneumonia. She stayed home, resting on the sofa, always under the watchful eye of Kathryn or Jack or someone in the family. Despite visits from a doctor, her health quickly deteriorated, and when she died, Jack was as grief-stricken as anyone.

In her grief my grandmother grew even closer to Jack and the rest of her children. Certainly my father sensed her vulnerability and wanted to spare her any more pain. I believe he felt that way toward her for her entire life. His letters home from war always painted a picture of serenity and good cheer, no matter how terrible the reality must have been. And that attitude was probably why, at age nineteen and about to be drafted, he devised a plan to enlist in the Navy and avoid land battle.

His plan, he was sure, would allow him to be of service but to stay far from flying bullets—whatever it took to keep him out of harm's way. Little did he realize that enlisting in the Navy would lead him directly into one of history's bloodiest battles.

Franklin Sousley: Hilltop, Kentucky

In the mountains of eastern Kentucky, the Sousley family roots go deep. Descendants of the English who settled here in the eighteenth century, they were mostly farming people, all the way down to Duke Sousley, who married Goldie Mitchell, a pretty girl with permed red hair, in November 1922. They set about the hard but productive life of raising tobacco outside the village of Hilltop.

Their first son, Malcolm, came ten months later, then Franklin with his Huck Finn red hair on September 19, 1925. The family home was a cabin, four small rooms heated by a pot-bellied stove. They had no electricity or plumbing. When Franklin was just three, five-year-old Malcolm suffered a ruptured appendix and died in Goldie's arms.

This left Franklin as the only son. Not unlike what happened to my own father when his sister died, Franklin's mother drew closer to him in her grief. As the boy grew, she took him along with her as she indulged in her favorite pastime—fishing in the Licking River.

When he was old enough, Franklin attended the two-room schoolhouse in nearby Elizaville. In May of 1933, when he was almost eight, Franklin greeted the arrival of his newborn brother, Julian. The occasion might have been a happier one but for his father's plight. The onset of diabetes in Duke led to a rapid deterioration of his health, and he died only a year after Julian was born. Franklin, just nine, found himself the man of the family, with a mother to comfort continually and a tiny brother to help care for.

The special mother-son bond between Goldie and Franklin deepened. Goldie, only in her early thirties, had already lost a son and a husband, but she didn't mope. She displayed a stubborn optimism, the will to go on that was transferred to Franklin. Goldie didn't smother her son in sadness, but encouraged him to revel in life's joys. And Franklin took the lesson to heart.

With a busy life, up early for school and to bed late at night after the chores, it seemed he had little time for play, but Franklin Sousley made the most of it. The strongest impression he left with his friends is that of a fun-loving, playful, daring boy. His close friend J. B. Shannon remembers Franklin as "a big freckle-faced boy with bright red hair. A rambunctious young man, not afraid of anyone."

World War II hovered in the background of Franklin's boyhood. News of its great battles and gossip about the fates of local servicemen filled the air at Hilltop as he cavorted and studied and helped Goldie in her struggles with the farm. There is no indication that Franklin paid the war much attention. He was far more interested in escorting Marion Hamm to church, to the movies, or just for a walk in the woods.

Upon graduating from high school, however, Franklin Sousley also had to be concerned with finding a way to shore up his struggling mother's finances. He went to work at a refrigerator plant in Dayton, Ohio, living in an inexpensive apartment. Eighteen-year-old Franklin was sending money back home to Goldie from his paycheck when, in January 1944, he was drafted. On that day, rather than accept his fate as an Army infantryman, Franklin Sousley made up his mind to become a U.S. Marine.

It had been a jolt for Goldie when Franklin had gone off to Dayton, farther away from Hilltop than she had ever traveled.

Now her son, who had smiled his way throughout his difficult boyhood, was headed to another world—and to war.

Harlon Block: Rio Grande Valley, Texas

Harlon was from a place that locals call simply "the Valley"— the Rio Grande Valley at the bottom of Texas, the far eastern end. The athletic young man was born on a farm outside of the small town of McAllen.

The farm had been something of a compromise between Harlon's parents, Ed Block and the former Ada Belle Brantley. Ed and Belle had been married in San Antonio in 1917, and Ed promptly went off to fight in France in World War I.

When Ed returned, he and Belle gave city life a try. Ed sold real estate and was moderately successful. But he dreamed of farming. One day he saw a flyer touting the Rio Grande Valley and claiming that a land boom was about to explode. Ed bought forty acres sight unseen. Belle was skeptical, but Ed painted a picture of ground-floor opportunity. In the end she gave her young husband the benefit of the doubt and agreed to go along with him. It would be the first of many compromises for Belle.

There was no industry in the Valley during the Depression; everyone was involved in agriculture, working the soil. The Blocks struggled at first. Their newly built farmhouse caught fire and burned to the ground. Ed had to take a job as a laborer and rent a small house while they got back on their feet. Belle had an idea to make some money. She suggested they buy a cow every two months with Ed's earnings. Before long the Blocks were in the dairy business.

Soon they had a family. Ed junior arrived in 1920, followed by Maurine two years later and Harlon in 1924. Later came three more boys, Larry, Corky, and Melford.

As a middle child in a large family, Harlon didn't have to be a trailblazer. He could follow along in his older siblings' footsteps. As he grew, he became an indispensable part of the dairy farm operation, helping his brothers and sisters milk the cows. Then Ed senior would be off on his route, selling the milk for five cents a quart.

Belle was determined to do right by her family, and she tried to be happy on the farm. But it was difficult for her. She missed the city and her friends there. Perhaps it was Belle's longing for another life that made her open to the preachings of the Seventh-Day Adventist Church. Shortly after their move to the Valley, Belle became a practitioner of the Protestant sect that strictly followed the Ten Commandments, including "Thou shalt not kill."

All Christians shared a belief in that commandment, but the Seventh-Day Adventists took it to heart. Adventist boys were taught they must never carry guns or knives because the Lord would offer them all the protection they needed. And Seventh-Day Adventists had a long record of refusing to fight in time of war. They never faltered in their support of their country, but most often they served in the medical corps as conscientious objectors.

Harlon was the child most influenced by Belle and her beliefs. He grew up feeling sure of what was right and wrong. He accepted that the Bible was the literal word of God, the Ten Commandments an absolute guide. But, in one of the contradictions of his character, he was also a free spirit. Often when his chores were finished he was off racing horses bareback. Seeking a better future, the Blocks soon moved to the neighboring town of Weslaco, a flat, square speculator's grid slapped down on the Valley floor. Ed bought a truck and began hauling crude oil from the fields to a nearby refinery. By this time Harlon had become more of a free spirit than ever. When Belle insisted that the Block children continue at the Adventist school back in McAllen, Harlon was the only one who refused to return. He felt he had absorbed all that the Adventists had to teach him. More important, he had matured physically and become interested in athletics, and the Adventist school did not have a sports program.

With his speed, broad shoulders, and muscular legs, Harlon decided he wanted to make his mark in the sport that attracted the local crowds and created excitement in Weslaco, and indeed in all of Texas: football.

Harlon wanted to be in on the action, part of a team. Belle didn't like such talk. She felt Harlon should make an effort to get back into the Adventist school. And football! Well, football was a game of violence, and the games were on Friday night, the beginning of the Sabbath, so football was out of the question.

Belle presented her views forcefully to Harlon, who shrugged noncommittally. She next appealed to Ed to discipline their stubborn son, but Ed backed off. Perhaps he simply wanted his son to excel at sports. There was also a special bond between Ed and Harlon, one of those intuitive connections that are not easily broken.

As his sons matured, Ed got every one of them involved in hauling crude oil from the hill-country wells to the refinery in McAllen. When Harlon was old enough—before he was old enough, Belle thought—Ed enlisted him as one of his drivers. It was exhausting work, but he and his father grew ever closer—"best friends," as Ed would later say.

Ed loved nothing more than Harlon's company, and he was torn when their months of working together drew to a close and Harlon returned to school. But he couldn't wait to cheer his most athletic son on the gridiron.

Harlon's developing brawn made him a natural for the Weslaco High football squad. He put in long hours of practice and made the starting team as punter, receiver, and blocking back. The Weslaco Panthers went on to an undefeated season. Harlon loved being part of a team. Although this was his first year at Weslaco, he made the All–South Texas team that season.

All the while Belle was fearful for her son's spirituality. He was playing around too much; he was always gone, Belle complained to Ed, who, like their son, was inclined to shrug and do nothing. Harlon was a difficult teenager in Belle's eyes, but he was pretty tame by most people's standards. He was bashful in groups and blushed at off-color jokes. His friend Leo Ryan said Harlon worried about his looks and never thought the girls liked him.

But the girls sensed something special in Harlon. His brother Ed junior told me that the girls flocked to Harlon. Harlon's favorite girl, the one many think he might have married after the war, was Catherine Pierce. "We'd go to the movies together," Catherine remembered. "And we'd go to church functions. We liked each other, we dated, but we never so much as held hands."

Harlon would soon be off to war, soon be a symbol to the world of a warrior. But it's doubtful that before he left Harlon Block ever kissed a girl.

Ira Hayes: Gila River Indian Reservation, Arizona

By the summer of 1998 I had already interviewed many people about Ira Hayes—his school chums, ex-Marines, his three living relatives—but I still felt I didn't know what had made him tick. I drove south out of Phoenix and was soon on the Pearl Harbor Highway, as Interstate 10 is called as it nears Ira's reservation. I drove through the dry, silent heat along flat pink desert land, a plain of mesquite bushes and deep green saguaro cactus that recedes until it hits the Santan Mountains.

I gazed out at Ira's land, the Gila River Indian Reservation. It's not big, with maybe fifteen thousand inhabitants. Behind me, although it's been dry for decades, was the waterless riverbed that is called the Gila River, next to a busy highway.

Ira was a Pima Indian, a member of a small, proud tribe that had inhabited this quiet land for centuries. He was born Ira Hamilton Hayes on January 12, 1923, to Nancy and Jobe Hayes. He was the eldest of the six Hayes children. Two children, Harold and Arlene, died as babies. Two other children died before they were thirty.

At birth Ira was already "apart," separated from other Americans by law and custom. Arizona, a state for only eleven years at the time of Ira's birth, did not recognize Pima Indians as citizens. Pimas could not vote; they could not sue anyone in the courts.

Ira was born into a one-room adobe hut. Sturdy and economical, it faced east in the traditional Pima way, so that each morning its occupants, opening the door, were greeted by the rising sun. An American flag graced one wall; religious paintings and a Bible were always in evidence.

Jobe Hayes was a cotton farmer and a man of few words. "He was a quiet man," Ira's niece Sara Bernal remembered of Jobe. "He would go days without saying anything unless you spoke to him first." And Kenny Hayes, Ira's only living brother, who himself rarely speaks, said only: "My dad hardly ever talked."

As a little boy, as a young man, and later as an adult, Ira was just like his dad. According to people I talked to, Ira could be in another's presence for hours without talking, silent as the mountains overlooking his reservation. His favorite card game was solitaire.

Yet when Ira did speak he displayed a keen mind and an impressive grasp of the English language. His mother, Nancy, a devout Presbyterian, read to him from the Bible when he was a child. All his life Ira devoured all kinds of books. He was the most prolific letter writer of the six flag raisers. And when it was time for high school Nancy sent Ira and her other children as boarders to the Phoenix Indian School.

Ira's tribe, the Pima, had lived for over two thousand years as successful and peaceful farmers. Unwarlike and rarely invaded, Pima Indians were a sharing people who offered their bounties to other nations and, in time, to the forty-niners and other whites making their way across the desert in prairie schooners, headed for California.

This generosity may have been a huge mistake. It drew attention to the paradise the tribe had painstakingly created for itself. In return for the Pimas' kindness and even protection under attacks by hostile Apaches, the migrating Easterners began to help themselves to the water from the Gila River, which at that time flowed strong and full. It wasn't long before the Gila's water level began to fall. By 1930 the great Gila River was little more than a trickle.

The remarkable thing, I thought, given the decades of thievery and abuse suffered by the Pimas, is that they maintained their character and dignity. In 1917, even though they were not U.S. citizens and were thus exempt from military service, a majority of young Pima men waived this right and enlisted to fight in France. Matthew Juan, a Pima, was the first Arizona soldier killed in action in World War I, a fact of which all Pima young men were proud.

In time Ira's school day would begin with news of faraway battles. "Every morning in school," classmate Eleanor Pasquale remembers, "we would get a report on World War Two. We would sing the anthems of the Army, the Marines, and the Navy."

Ira enlisted in the Marines nine months after Pearl Harbor, when he nineteen. His community sent him off to war with a traditional Pima ceremony. There was a bountiful feast, and each guest spoke to Ira about honor, loyalty, his family, and his people. The Pima disliked war and all its brutality, but in this instance, the elders agreed, it was necessary. A choir sang hymns, and everyone embraced young Ira and said a private good-bye. All prayed for his safety.

Rene Gagnon: Manchester, New Hampshire

Rene arrived in the world on March 7, 1925, the only child of French Canadian mill workers Henry and Irene Gagnon. In those years French Canadians formed a dense ethnic enclave on the west side of Manchester, New Hampshire, a "Little Canada" in which French was the language and Catholicism the religion.

Strikingly handsome with his lean Gallic face and dark hair and brows, Rene grew up under the coddling influence of Irene, who divorced Henry while the boy was still a toddler. Irene's life consisted of her job in the mills and her son. She often brought Rene to work with her to show him off, to be cooed over by the other women. He attended a Catholic grade school and was a decent student but did little to distinguish himself.

Rene probably didn't reflect on it, but he grew up in the final years of Manchester's century-long domination of an industry. Throughout the nineteenth century, the textile mills of Manchester, about fifty miles north of Boston, drew swarms of workers from the East Coast as well as from French-speaking rural Canada. Everything—work and social life—revolved around the mills. These rural men and women (and their children) took for granted the social regimentation of their lives; they accepted the notion that a kind of unseen but always attentive power ruled over them.

When Rene was old enough, he worked alongside his mother and other women in the same vast room. The handsome boy was almost always the center of attention. After two years of high school, he dropped out altogether so that he could work full time next to his mother and her friends.

But there were other women there, younger girls who were attracted to the dark, handsome boy. Irene was particularly concerned by a young, aggressive girl who had her eye on Rene. Her name was Pauline Harnois, and she seemed to cast a spell over Rene, ready to take control away from Irene. Like a leaf in a river, Rene was swept along with whatever current took him, and he spent more time with Pauline than Irene liked.

One December afternoon, when Rene was sixteen, he and a bunch of the guys were listening to a football game on the radio when the program was interrupted. The Japanese had, without warning, bombed and sunk our ships at Pearl Harbor, Hawaii.

The next day the Manchester *Union-Leader* paperboys were brandishing editions whose headline was just one word: "WAR!"

Rene Gagnon listened to this news, read about it, shrugged, and went back to the mill and his mother and Pauline Harnois. It was all beyond his control. He kept on working. Life went on: the mill, his mother, Pauline, the bright lights along Elm Street.

Rene Gagnon kept on working right up until his Army draft notice arrived in May 1943. Then he enlisted in the Marines and submitted to yet another large, outside influence that would mold his life.

Irene didn't want to lose her boy, but she thought it would do him good to get away from Pauline. What Rene didn't tell his mother was that he had already made a fateful decision. At the age of seventeen he comforted the sad Pauline with the promise that he would marry her when he returned from the war.

Mike Strank: Franklin Borough, Pennsylvania

At age twenty-four Mike was the "old man" of his company, the oldest of the flag raisers—and the one larger-than-life hero. When old comrades talk to me about Mike they become young

24

men again. "A Marine's Marine" is the phrase they all get to sooner or later. They speak of the strapping man, a fearless, selfless warrior. Yet what men valued about Mike Strank—what makes their spines stiffen in admiration fifty years after the battle—was his leadership. That, and his quality of compassion.

"Follow me," Sergeant Mike used to tell the boys in his squad, "and I'll try to bring all of you back safely to your mothers. Listen to me, and follow my orders, and I'll do my best to bring you home."

He was born Mychal Strenk on November 10, 1919, into a poor family in a small farm town in Czechoslovakia. The following year his father, Vasil, immigrated to America and changed his last name to Strank. Seeking a decent salary, he settled in the small Pennsylvania steel town of Franklin Borough. Central to the town's existence were the Bethlehem steel mills and iron mines that employed thousands of workers.

Vasil worked the mines for three years before he could send for his wife, Martha, and the baby, Mychal, who came to America in 1922. By the end of that year, Mychal, who was renamed Michael, had a baby brother, John. A few years later Pete would follow, with sister Mary still eight years in the future.

The family lived in a two-room rental apartment inside the Slavic enclave of Franklin Borough. The rooms were a kitchen and a bedroom. To Martha especially, this was luxury: a castle, she said, compared with what they had had in Czechoslovakia. Vasil trudged off to the mine at three o'clock every afternoon. He wore the same clothes all year round, with frequent washings to rid them of the black coal dust. But no one complained. This was progress! The Strank family was optimistic about their economic future in their new homeland, while maintaining the values of the tightly knit Slavic community.

Without realizing it, Vasil Strank might have begun the molding of his eldest son into a Marine's Marine at an early age. The family maintained a strict Old World value system—when one of the boys had misbehaved, Martha would report it to Vasil upon his return home at night, and the next day he would wake up early, when the boys did, to administer punishment.

Vasil insisted on a special rule for this punishment: No matter which boy had committed the offense, all three would be disciplined equally. In this way, Vasil thought, he could transfer the burden of discipline from himself to the boys and make them see that they had a shared interest in the good behavior of each.

This, probably without Vasil's knowing it, is one of the fundamental principles of military training and in particular Marine training, where young men are taught to forget their individuality and are remolded into a member of a team. Shared responsibility—being part of a unit—is essential to survival in combat.

As the eldest of the three brothers and the brightest—his intellectual skills would soon blaze brilliantly to the surface—not only did Mike grasp the concept of teamwork and equal responsibility, but he became a connection between his father and his two younger siblings. In short, he became a sergeant.

While Vasil provided the discipline, it was Mike's mother who taught him about love and faith. Like Jack Bradley, Mike was close to his mother and absorbed her Catholic faith. Before bed each night, he and his two brothers would kneel on the floor before a vivid painting of the Last Supper and say their evening prayers in Slovak. They looked out for one another. They took to making sure they wore the same color shirt to school each day, like uniforms.

Raised in the Slovak tongue, Mike did not know English when he began first grade. By the end of the year Mike was so proficient in his new language that he skipped second grade. It was amazing, his relatives said: The boy never forgot anything. He could open the evening newspaper, read a page of it, and the next morning tell you exactly what all the articles said.

He was shy around girls, but then, not many of the boys in Franklin Borough were at ease with girls, or vice versa. Men he understood. And men liked and understood Mike Strank.

It seemed that the warm, supportive, and structured life of the Strank family would never come undone. But as the Depression began to sink its teeth into eastern Pennsylvania, the steel mills, like the rest of America, began to shut down. There was no future here for Mike.

He ended up as part of a brainstorm of President Roosevelt to get the country back on its economic feet: the Civilian Conservation Corps (CCC). Through the 1930s youthful CCC workers planted millions of trees across America, released nearly a billion game fish into the country's rivers and lakes, and dug thousands of miles of canals for irrigation and transportation.

But the CCC had a greater function—one that did not fully reveal itself until America went to war. It served as training for some three million boys, many of whom would flood into the armed services after Pearl Harbor. Administered by the Army, the CCC introduced its recruits to camp life, to military discipline, to physical fitness, and to a sense of loyalty to comrades and to a cause.

Mike disappeared into the CCC in 1937 weighing 140

pounds. He came out two years later a strapping 180, tanned and handsome. Mike was nineteen now. The year was 1939. In Europe Hitler's legions were overrunning his Czech homeland, making slaves of his people.

Mike decided to join the Marines.

He didn't have to do it. He could have avoided military service altogether, given his Czech citizenship. His brother John always puzzled over the fact that the Marines allowed him in at all; apparently no one checked out his nationality.

Mike enlisted on October 6, 1939. And soon the brainy Czech boy would transform himself into the ultimate American fighting man: a tough, driven, and confident leader.

THREE

America's War

What kind of people do they think we are? Is it possible they do not realize that we shall never cease to persevere against them until they have been taught a lesson which they and the world will never forget?

—Winston Churchill on the Japanese, 1942

A sleepy American Sunday afternoon in early December 1941, Yuletide season in the air, roast chicken dinners finished, and the dishes washed. Television had not been invented, so families sat around listening to the radio for news and entertainment. Suddenly an urgent bulletin crackled through the static on the family radio.

"The Japanese have attacked Pearl Harbor, Hawaii, by air!"

The following day, as many as eighty million listeners, including hundreds of thousands of children, tuned in again to hear President Franklin Roosevelt deliver a six-and-a-half-minute speech whose key phrases would never be forgotten.

Yesterday, December 7, 1941—a date which will live in infamy—the United States of America was suddenly and deliberately attacked by naval and air forces of the Empire of Japan. . . . With confidence in our armed forces, with the unbounding determination of our people, we will gain the inevitable triumph, so help us God!

Before Pearl Harbor, America had looked across the Atlantic for an enemy. Adolf Hitler was the enemy we feared, and Japan was dismissed as a less significant threat. But after the "day of infamy" newspaper maps of the Pacific and Asia were scrutinized at the kitchen tables of America.

Now America was in a world war, a "two-ocean war." Across the Atlantic, in Europe, the United States would be fighting in support of and with the Allies. Against Japan, however, America would stand virtually alone in the Pacific. Japan had attacked American soil, and the first and last American battles of World War II would be fought on Japanese soil. The Pacific war would be "America's war."

America went to war in December 1941. The Europeans had been fighting since 1939. But for millions of Asians, World War II had begun a decade before, in 1931, when Japan invaded Manchuria, part of China—a U.S. ally. To consolidate its control of Manchuria, Japan attacked and invaded other parts of China six years later.

By 1941 Japan, with a committed citizenry, an experienced army, and an immense navy, became so confident that it could control the entire Pacific that it launched a surprise attack on Pearl Harbor. The goal of the Japanese military was to cripple the U.S. Navy. This way, the Japanese generals and admirals reasoned, the United States would never be able to stop Japanese conquests.

And America's boys were spoiling for revenge. Robert Leader, who later served with John Bradley in Company E, recalled his anger on that shocking Sunday afternoon: "We were so mad at the Japanese for bombing Pearl Harbor. They bombed on a Sunday, we went to school on Monday, and they piped in President Roosevelt's 'date of infamy' speech. A bunch of us boys got together and said, 'Let's join up!' " Hundreds of thousands of young Americans were just as angry as Bob Leader, and enlistment centers were soon overwhelmed by eager boys and men.

By the summer of 1942 the Japanese military had conquered a swath of territory with the same confidence and ease that Adolf Hitler displayed in Europe. It was with particular alarm that on July 4, 1942, American reconnaissance planes discovered that the Japanese were building an airstrip on Guadalcanal, an island near the southern tip of the Solomon Islands, to the northeast of Australia. An entrenched Japanese force there would spell disaster for Australia and its allies in the South Pacific.

America knew it had to draw the line on this dangerous southern thrust. But who would take a stand? The American, British, and Chinese armies had been defeated by Japan's Imperial Army. The Japanese appeared to be supermen, impossible to stop.

It was at this critical stage that the United States Marine Corps came onto the scene. The Marines had been on the fringes of the American armed forces and had never played a significant role in American military history. As recently as the

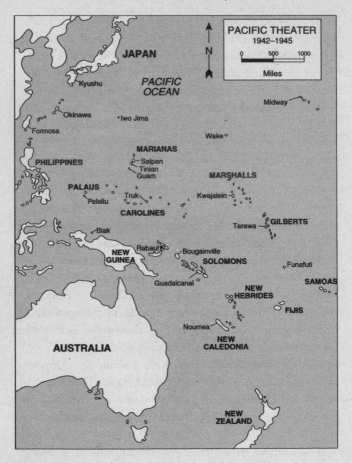

spring of 1940 the Marines had numbered only twenty-five thousand enlisted men.

In the early 1920s a veteran Marine officer of World War I

named Holland M. "Howlin' Mad" Smith assembled a team of officers to rethink the Marines' mission. Smith suggested that a great many American boys must be trained to master more-exacting combat skills, including the concept of amphibious warfare: troops disembarking from large ships, then speeding in smaller landing craft, often under fire, toward enemy beaches. Once on land the Marines, armed with rifles, grenades, and flamethrowers, would destroy a well-entrenched enemy.

Over two decades Howlin' Mad Smith and his staff created, refined, and rehearsed the modern science of amphibious warfare. He reshaped the modern Marine Corps. There were four Army divisions in the South Pacific when the urgency arose for an amphibious expedition to seize Guadalcanal. But this battle called for the best-trained amphibious warriors in the world. The Marines waded onto Guadalcanal on August 7, 1942. Caught by surprise, the Japanese did not at first oppose their landing. The Marines streamed in and unloaded their supplies until the Japanese navy finally counterattacked. After losing four ships, the U.S. Navy fled. The Marines ashore were abandoned, standing alone against an enemy that had never been defeated.

For weeks these isolated Marines fought off attacks by Japanese ground troops as Japanese air and naval power struck at them day after day. Fighting against seemingly impossible odds, living on two meals a day of captured Japanese rice, the Marines secured the island by December. Some twenty-three thousand Japanese were killed; another thirteen thousand fled the island.

The Marines had stunned the Japanese and handed the Imperial Army their first military defeat of the war. But for the Marines

Guadalcanal revealed a disquieting truth: America's war with the Japanese would be fought on the most primitive level. It was to be a brutal, all-out struggle for total domination. The Japanese fighting man believed he was fighting in the proud tradition of ancient samurai. Bushido, the "way of the warrior," had for centuries been the honored code of Japan's proud samurai caste. In the past the samurai had been a small elite group within the larger society. But in the early 1900s the Japanese military set forth an updated version of Bushido. Its aim was to make warriors of the entire male populace. Death in battle was portrayed as an honor to the family and a heroic act on the part of the individual. Surrender was a disgrace to the soldier and his family.

The twentieth-century Japanese generals taught a cult of death. The young men the Japanese military drew into its ranks were, in effect, brainwashed to believe that by laying down their lives they were walking in the footsteps of heroic samurai.

Not surprisingly, the military hierarchy had little respect for the men they brainwashed. They referred to army draftees as *issen gorin*, which meant "one yen, five rin," the cost of mailing a draft-notice postcard—less than a penny. Weapons and horses were treated with care by the generals, but no second-class private was as valuable as an animal.

Unable to surrender, forced to fight to the death, the young Japanese soldier had no respect for Americans who didn't do the same. So a tragedy occurred in the Pacific—a tragedy brought about by the Japanese military leaders who forced their brutalized young men to be brutal themselves.

. . .

Back in America, the dramatic Marine victory on Guadal-canal fired the imagination and patriotism of American boys. The Marines had suddenly become the branch of choice for anyone who wanted the toughest combat possible. Unlike the Army, the Marines didn't draft anyone. You had to volunteer. And the Marines didn't take just any volunteer. You had to be one of the best. Many boys were washed out during boot camp.

Boot camp usually lasted eight weeks and had the purpose not only of teaching combat skills and discipline, but of mold-ing young individuals into team players. Many young men en-tered the Marines with dreams of being heroes, but Marine leaders quickly taught a different lesson: Battles are won by teams working together, by sacrifice, by *not* trying to stand out.

There was another reason for focusing on the team and not your friends. "Don't get close to anybody," the drill instructor would warn his charges. "Because every other one of you is probably gonna get killed!"

In basic training the boys were growing fit, learning marks-manship and weaponry and chain of command, learning to live in alternating states of boredom and lethal urgency. All mili-taries harden their recruits, bend young men to their will. But the Marine Corps provides its members with a secret weapon. The Navy has its ships, the Air Force has its planes, the Army its detailed doctrine, but culture—the values and assumptions that shape its members—distinguishes the Marines. The Marines call their culture "esprit de corps."

This was a warrior class, the Marine Corps, but a very differ-ent one from Japanese soldiers. Both wanted to win, both were disciplined and well trained, both knew the meaning of courage

35

and sacrifice. But one side believed in fighting blindly to its death for a remote, almost abstract authority—the emperor, the state, the Land of the Rising Sun. The other culture, the United States Marines, fought out of love for each other, for their country, and for the proud spirit known as esprit de corps.

FOUR

Call of Duty

Those who expect to reap the blessings of liberty
must undergo the fatigues of supporting it.

—Thomas Paine

On the day Japanese bombs surprised the sailors at Pearl Harbor there was a six-year spread among those who would later raise the flag on Iwo Jima.

Pennsylvanian Mike Strank was the oldest at twenty-one, already a Marine corporal with two years of service. The Pima Indian, Ira Hayes, was an eighteen-year-old sophomore at the Phoenix Indian School with eight months to go before he enlisted in the Marines. Six months younger than Ira, Jack Bradley was a recent high school graduate and apprenticing his way to a Wisconsin funeral director's license. Harlon Block was seventeen, still a school year away from his senior gridiron heroics for the Weslaco Panthers. Franklin Sousley was a sixteen-year-old junior in high school, rushing home to do his chores. Rene Gagnon was only fifteen, in his second and last year of high school, soon to melt into the routine of New Hampshire mill life.

Mike Strank got to the war first. He had enlisted on October 6, 1939—the only one of the six flag raisers to sign up before America entered the war. He plowed through boot camp at Parris Island, South Carolina, thriving on the routine and loving this rough-and-tumble world.

Private First Class Strank sailed first to Guantánamo Bay, Cuba, for additional training in January 1941. America was at peace, but the Marines had been practicing amphibious assaults in the Caribbean islands for over sixteen years by now.

By April Corporal Strank was back at Parris Island, and he later began molding other young Marines at New River, North Carolina (now Camp Lejeune). He became Sergeant Strank two months after Pearl Harbor. By June 1942, after a short leave to visit his family in Pennsylvania, he was headed for combat.

But Mike was not going to Europe as he had hoped, to help avenge his ravaged Czech homeland. Instead he joined the great swarm of young American men hastily assembled, trained, armed, and rushed west to stem the Japanese onslaught.

At about the same time as Mike headed for the Pacific, Ira Hayes was in Marine boot camp near San Diego, California. No one quite knew what thoughts and motivations inspired this quiet boy, but his mother, Nancy, remembered Ira's determination to be a Marine: "We wanted him to stay. But he brought home his papers and we signed them. He said he wanted to go and defend us."

Ira excelled in boot camp. No matter how demanding the training, Ira wrote home that he enjoyed it. When he completed boot camp he applied for and was accepted for parachute training. Jumping out of airplanes in 1942 was a challenging and dangerous business. Marine parachute school accepted only the best candidates. On November 30, 1942, he earned his USMC paratrooper wings—the first Pima to graduate from parachute training. Shortly thereafter "Chief Falling Cloud," as his buddies dubbed him, was assigned to Company B, Third Parachute Battalion, Divisional Special Troops, Third Marine Division.

The Marines photographed Ira crouched with his parachute, ready to jump out of a plane. The photo caused a sensation back home when it appeared in the Pima *Gazette* and the Phoenix Indian School *Redskin*. "We were all proud of him. He made us proud to be Pimas," Ira's friend Eleanor Pasquale remembered.

But no one was more proud of his new elite status than Ira himself. A glow seemed to fill him, perhaps because for the first time in his life he was accomplishing something, and he began signing letters home "Paratrooper, PFC I. H. Hayes."

The summer and fall of 1942 had been eventful on fronts far distant from the football fields of south Texas. In August, about the time Harlon Block was drawing on his pads and helmet, massive American air attacks began in Europe, and German planes pulverized Stalingrad, Russia.

The North African invasion began in November, around homecoming time for Harlon. And in the South Pacific the Marines' stunning victory at Guadalcanal—the first American land battle of World War II—would ignite new waves of patriotism and fighting fervor among American boys.

It certainly ignited the Weslaco High Panthers. During their winning season in the fall of 1942, someone on the team had the idea for all of the seniors on the team to enlist in the Marine Corps together after they graduated in May. Did Harlon have any qualms about war? Given his upbringing as a Seventh-Day Adventist, he might have struggled internally with this dilemma—but he didn't express it to friends.

When Harlon told Belle and Ed that he was going to enlist in the Marines along with his football buddies, it was Belle who was most distressed. She pleaded with Harlon to enter the medical service, to avoid the killing. As a Seventh-Day Adventist, Harlon had a legitimate out; he didn't have to fight.

But at Weslaco High School there were no forces to support his Adventist background. Just the opposite—peer pressure was pushing Harlon hard to join up. Because he was underage, however, and needed at least one parent's permission to enlist, he asked Belle for her cooperation. When she refused, Harlon turned to Ed. Always supportive of his son's wishes and judgment, Ed had little hesitation—for which Belle no doubt did not readily forgive her husband.

In January 1943 a photo appeared in the local newspaper of thirteen Weslaco Panthers lined up facing Marine Captain D. M. Taft, taking their oath to serve their country. A recruiter had promised them that the entire team would be able to stick together in the Corps.

Belle might have been scared to death for her boy, but Harlon showed no fear or worry. At boot camp near San Diego, Harlon, like Mike and Ira, excelled in his training. He took to wearing his helmet at a cocky angle and made friends easily. Like Ira, he went on to para-trooper school and earned his wings. In some ways training was all too easy for Harlon. He felt he was ready for combat and didn't like waiting around. On November 15, 1943, Harlon got his wish and shipped out in the wakes of Mike and Ira.

In his first Pacific duty Mike Strank was assigned to a Marine unit called the Raiders. It was considered the toughest outfit in the Pacific. The Raiders introduced "gung ho" into the American fighting lexicon. Theirs was the original mission impossible: to storm beaches considered inaccessible in advance of larger forces; to launch rapid, surprise raids with light arms against an enemy that always outnumbered them; and to roam behind enemy lines for long periods, cut off from their own command.

The Pacific ground war was largely a strategy of island hopping. The first island invaded by the Marines was Guadal-canal; the second, with Mike and the Raiders leading the assault, was Bougainville. Here the Marines encountered a green maze of well-camouflaged enemy along with millions of biting insects, impenetrable jungle, seemingly bottomless mangrove swamps, and man-eating crocodiles. To be a Marine on Bougainville meant a miserable existence of being wet, cold, exhausted, and always in danger of being picked off by a Japanese sniper.

Air attacks on the island began in August of 1943 and con-tinued through the fall. Diversionary landings on nearby islands occurred in October as distant Marine units hurried to the area, drawing a circle around Bougainville so no supplies or reinforce-ments could get to the Japanese.

Among the arrivals were Ira Hayes, who landed at Vella Lavella in October, and Harlon Block, who hit New Caledonia four days before Christmas. For both these boys, their hard-won paratrooper wings were now matters of ancient history. What they would experience on the island of Bougainville would change their lives forever.

As the Pacific conflict began to take shape, a mild-mannered young man in Appleton, Wisconsin, was preparing to do his duty. Jack Bradley was nineteen in January 1943. Two years out of high school, he had just completed an eighteen-month apprenticeship in the mortuary arts. But it was clear that he would be drafted at any moment.

Jack's father urged him to join the Navy, avoiding the dirty business of fighting in trenches, in pouring rain, on an empty stomach. The Navy was cleaner and more efficient, his dad said, and best of all, Jack wouldn't have to worry about handling a rifle.

On January 13, 1943, my father and a friend, Bob Connelly, signed up with the U.S. Navy. Jack was hopeful that the Navy would take one look at his mortician apprenticeship and assign him to a relatively safe position, such as pharmacist's assistant.

By February, after several stops, Jack and Bob found themselves at the Navy's training center at Farragut, Idaho. In March, to his great surprise, Jack was told he'd been selected to become a Seabee—the Navy engineering cadre that often did its road-building and railroad-repairing work under hostile fire.

"Your dad stormed into the office and demanded to know why," Bob Connelly recalled to me. "They told him it was because he was color-blind. Why they wanted color-blind Seabees, your father never could figure out, but he hit the roof. From what he knew, the Seabees fought on land. He told them, 'I'm not color-blind! I had a beer last night! Test me again!' "

Jack Bradley got his wish. He was not required to join the Seabees. However, this bit of luck (or maybe fate), which Jack thought would keep him far from the front lines, ensured he would later fight in the worst battle in the history of the Marine Corps.

But Jack had some good duty in front of him. In the fall of 1943, about the time Harlon sailed for the South Pacific, Jack Bradley was transferred to Oaknoll Naval Hospital in Oakland, California. His job was to take care of wounded soldiers from the Pacific campaigns.

He was new to this work, but to his fellow seventeen- and eighteen-year-old corpsmen he showed a certain maturity. People began to call him "Doc." Jack thought he had it made, working with the doctors and nurses in clean, ordered rooms. And San Francisco beckoned just across the bay for weekend getaways. It seemed like the good life in the midst of a very bad war.

Rene Gagnon joined the Marines in May of 1943. It was two months after his seventeenth birthday. Why the Marines instead of the Army for Rene? He was motivated not by esprit de corps, not by feelings of revenge against the Japanese, not even by patriotism particularly. He had spotted a Marine recruiting poster and was knocked out by the uniform, by those snazzy dress blues and whites. His attitude, a friend recalled, was: "I'm goin' in anyway. So I may as well look good."

After secretly promising Pauline he would come back and marry her, Rene was sent to Parris Island, where Mike Strank had trained. Rene did well enough to make private first class. In July 1943 he was transferred to the Marine guard company at the Charleston Navy yard in South Carolina. Like his civilian life, his Marine career seemed to be going nowhere in particular. That seemed just fine with Rene, who, when he did wear his dress uniform, looked as fine as any Marine in the land.

There are few direct accounts of what Mike, Ira, and Harlon experienced on Bougainville. We do know that Mike was there longest, fighting on what is always the single toughest day, D day—the first day of invasion. On November 1, 1943, along with fourteen thousand other Marines of the Third Division, Sergeant Mike Strank splashed ashore at dawn in high surf.

Mike and the other landing Marines were raked by a devastating cross fire of Japanese machine guns and artillery fire. The Japanese resistance there was far more concentrated than on Guadalcanal. The Marines could see no enemy. The Japanese were concealed by dense jungle foliage that spilled all the way down to the waterline. And they were protected by another type of shield that would recur from island to island in the Pacific campaign: concrete bunkers.

At Bougainville the preinvasion naval bombardment was supposed to have destroyed these bunker positions. But the Navy had played it too safe, launching some of the bombardment from a range of over seven miles and failing to wipe out the bunkers. And because of that, many young Marines were dying all around Mike. This must have been hard for him, the shepherd who wanted to bring everyone under his command back home alive.

. . .

Ira Hayes had enlisted in the Marines wanting to "protect his family," bursting with pride that had only deepened as he excelled in training. But as tough as he might be, at heart Ira was a passive boy, a quiet Pima. No one remembered him ever raising his voice, much less getting in a fight, though there were a few bursts of temper. Now Ira had to kill—not at a distance, as in target practice, but close up.

Ira landed on Bougainville in the early hours of December 3. In contrast to what Mike had experienced, Ira and his company walked onto the island unopposed, the enemy invisible and silent. However, this would quickly change.

One night, weaving through dense jungle on patrol, Ira and his Company K buddies found themselves in the midst of the enemy. Undiscovered but also outnumbered, everyone hid in foxholes, passing the night in an intense monsoon that left them cold and drenched. Ira and another Marine, Bill Faulkner, traded turns staying awake in their foxhole when the sleeping Faulkner was jolted awake by bloodcurdling screams.

Horrified, he tried to make sense of the violent lashings in the darkness. Under the cover of night, a Japanese soldier had crept soundlessly to the edge of the foxhole, and after a struggle, Ira killed him.

Ira found out firsthand what it was like fighting the Japanese in the Pacific. He had performed with courage and determination. But were the screams of dying men in his head now? All he would reveal in a letter to his mother from this miserable jungle was: "I'm okay, thanks to my Lord."

. . .

Harlon Block came to Bougainville on December 21, just days before the island was declared secure. There was still plenty of fighting, however. Arriving at a battle site known as "Hellzapoppin' Ridge," Harlon was suddenly in a macabre world of splintered trees and burned-out brush, shooting his rifle and getting fired upon. The earth around him became a mass of mud and dead bodies. The Seventh-Day Adventist was getting his first glimpse of the world's wickedness.

As the Marines tried to move forward, a Japanese machine gun stuttered and the enemy artillery roared, raking the American line. A Japanese counterattack slammed into the Marines' left flank. Harlon Block found himself in hand-to-hand combat. With knife, gun, and bare hands, the Texas pass catcher fought amid the confusion of English and Japanese screams.

When Harlon enlisted at the age of eighteen, he couldn't imagine the horror that lay behind the noble concepts of "fighting for your country" and "doing your duty." Now, as Harlon learned what his duty really was, the glory began to fade at the edges.

Something happened to Mike, Ira, and Harlon on Bougainville. They would never discuss it, never identify exactly what had affected them so. But for the rest of their days, death was never far from their thoughts. The three Pacific veterans sailed home from Bougainville on separate ships that left in the second week of January. They would have a month to stare at the ocean and ponder their private thoughts before they arrived in San Diego on February 14, 1944.

· · ·

At about this time, the lives of the six flag raisers were on parallel paths that would soon merge. Franklin Sousley was getting his first taste of life as a Marine. He had entered the Corps on January 5 and reported to the recruit depot in San Diego for boot camp. Across the country, eighteen-year-old Private First Class Rene Gagnon was serving in a military police unit guarding the Navy yard at Charleston, South Carolina. And Jack Bradley found himself transferred from the Oaknoll Navy Hospital in Oakland, California, to field medical school (FMS) outside San Diego.

For my father this was not good news. It meant he was being transferred to the Marines to be a combat medic, a corpsman. He must have been stunned. His strategy had been to join the Navy to avoid ground fighting. Now he found himself a member of the most rugged group of warriors in the world.

At FMS, Navy corpsmen were trained to care for Marines in battle. FMS had classes in specialized lifesaving skills, and Jack was also expected to endure the rigors of battle like any leatherneck. That meant tough Marine Corps conditioning. He now wore Marine uniforms and Marine dog tags; he rose at dawn to hike with Marines who never slowed down.

In February and March of 1944 Jack continued his FMS training, while Rene stayed back in South Carolina as an MP. Franklin was granted a furlough, or leave, after boot camp, as were Mike, Ira, and Harlon after they docked in San Diego from Bougainville.

Ira was back on the Gila reservation a few days after he touched land. At twenty, her boy was stockier now, Nancy noticed; he had gained about fifteen pounds of muscle during boot camp, and it had stayed on him during the jungle nightmare on Bougainville.

47

But the real change, his mother saw, was in his manner. He'd always had a solemn face, his full mouth in repose a natural frown until he smiled. But now those turned-down corners did not broaden so easily into even the faintest smile. Suddenly he looked downright sullen.

As Ira's leave drew to a close, at a farewell dinner with tribal elders he praised his fellow Marines for their bravery, self-sacrifice, and brotherhood. Ira concluded by promising never to bring any shame upon his tribe. When he finished speaking, they warmly embraced him. As a choir sang, Ira cried softly. And then he went back to war.

Mike Strank returned to Franklin Borough worn out by battle and by a case of malaria he had contracted on Bougainville. His friends Mike and Eva Slazich took him out for an evening on the town. They saw a movie, a war movie. Slazich asked his friend what he thought of the movie. Mike Strank remarked quietly: "It isn't really like that."

At the end of the evening Mike turned to his friend and said, "I doubt if I'll ever see you again. I don't think I'll be coming back."

"Don't say that!" replied a shocked Slazich.

A sense of his own mortality must have been equally hard for Mike to accept, but his family would never know. When Vasil asked if there was any way Mike could secure a training assignment in the States so they could see him more often, Mike replied, "Dad, there's a war going on out there. Young boys are fighting that war. And they need my help."

. . .

Harlon Block was also feeling his own mortality. Visiting family and friends on leave in Texas, he didn't say much to Ed and Belle, but to his favorite girl, Catherine Pierce, he confided his doubts. He surprised her as he softly said, "I don't think I'll be coming back, Catherine."

"He was a different person," Catherine told me. "Before he went to war he had been happy, with lots of enthusiasm. Now he was quiet, like something was weighing on him. I tried to encourage him. I said, Oh, Harlon, don't be silly. Nothing is going to happen to you.'"

Hilltop, Kentucky, came alive when their Marine, Franklin Sousley, arrived home on furlough. "When Franklin came home," his friend J. B. Shannon, then a wide-eyed thirteen-year-old, re-members, "it was a big deal for our little community. He stepped off the train in his Marine dress blues looking straight as a string."

On Franklin's last night home he had a date with Marion Hamm. "He came over to my house and we visited," she remembered. "We took a walk, and he told me how proud he was to be a Marine, how excited he was to serve his country in the Corps." At the end of the night he asked Marion to do what so many millions of World War II boys asked of their special girls: "He asked me to wait for him."

The next morning Franklin said his farewells to his friends and family. They embraced and cried. He presented his mother with a copy of his formal Marine Corps portrait. Then Franklin stepped back. With a big smile he looked Goldie in the eye and proclaimed, "Momma, I'm gonna do something to make you proud of me."

His last words to his sweetheart Marion were: "When I come back, I'll be a hero."

49

It was a battle on the tiny atoll of Tarawa in the central Pacific, north of Bougainville, that would foreshadow the fate of Mike, Harlon, Franklin, Ira, Rene, Doc, and all the Marines fighting America's war.

Tarawa was a tiny one-square-mile spit of sand, only eight hundred yards wide. Tarawa represented the kickoff of Howlin' Mad Smith's central Pacific thrust on the "road to Tokyo," the opening of a second front in the war against Japan. This was a new theater of sand, coral, and volcanic rock that left the jungles of the South Pacific far behind.

The Japanese had boasted that Tarawa "could not be taken in a thousand years." Howlin' Mad thought otherwise. Huge Navy gunships hit the well-fortified island with the greatest concentration of aerial bombardment and naval gunfire in the history of warfare up to that time.

But when the first wave of Marines stormed ashore on November 20, 1943, they found that the bombardment had been largely ineffective. Japanese gunfire ripped through the Marines' ranks. Confusion reigned as the Americans were pinned down.

Just when it seemed that things couldn't get worse, the landing boats with reinforcements hit an exposed reef five hundred yards from shore and were grounded. The Marines on board didn't hesitate. They jumped from their stranded craft into chest-deep water holding their arms and ammunition above their heads.

In one of the bravest scenes in the history of warfare, these Marines slogged through the deep water into sheets of machine-gun bullets. There was nowhere to hide. The Marines, almost wholly submerged and their hands full of equipment, could not defend themselves. But they kept coming. Bullets sliced through their ranks, killing over three hundred Marines in those long minutes.

The Marines overcame seemingly hopeless odds, and in three days of horrific fighting Tarawa was captured. The Marines suffered a shocking forty-four hundred casualties, but they destroyed the entire Japanese garrison of five thousand.

Tarawa was the first major amphibious assault in which the Marines faced sustained opposition on the beach. The American victory there opened the central Pacific to a new Marine thrust, with more difficult amphibious island assaults ahead. And it made clear to Marine commanders that many more motivated and well-trained Marines would be needed to win America's war in the Pacific.

So in March of 1944 the Marines issued new orders to six young boys. They were to report to a new camp to become part of a new Marine division. Destiny, and the great events in the Pacific, began to draw the six flag raisers toward one another.

FIVE

Forging the Spearhead

If the Army and the Navy
Ever look on heaven's scenes
They will find the streets are guarded
By United States Marines.

—from "The Marines' Hymn"

The flag raisers' new home was Camp Pendleton, south of Los Angeles.

At the camp an entirely new Marine division—the Fifth— would be activated on November 11, 1943, Armistice Day. The urgency surrounding its birth was dictated by harsh military realities. The battle of Tarawa had demonstrated the need for many more Marines trained to rout out well-entrenched Japanese defenders.

Mike, Harlon, and Ira reported to Camp Pendleton at the end of their post-Bougainville furloughs. Forty percent of this new force would be composed of veterans such as they. Doc, Franklin, and Rene represented the remaining 60 percent— young boys just out of basic training. Doc came up in April from his crash course at field medical school in San Diego.

Franklin arrived from boot camp in San Diego. Rene was shipped over from the camp at Charleston.

All six boys were assigned to Company E, nicknamed "Easy"—a stinging irony, given its fate. Easy Company consisted of about 250 men. They were divided into a headquarters (or command) section, three rifle platoons, a machine-gun platoon to supplement the rifle platoons, and a 60mm-mortar section to back up the riflemen. Doc was one of two corpsmen assigned to the Third Platoon, led by Lieutenant Keith Wells. (Corpsmen remained technically within the Navy but trained and lived with the men whom they would watch over in battle.)

Mike, Harlon, Franklin, and Ira were in the Second Platoon, led by Lieutenant Ed Pennel. Its forty members were divided into four squads. Sergeant Mike was a squad leader with three corporals reporting to him. One was Corporal Harlon Block, to whom Private First Class Franklin Sousley and Private First Class Ira Hayes in turn reported. Rene was in another of Mike's squads.

Easy Company's boss was tall, lean Wisconsin native Captain Dave Severance, a tough, ramrod-straight Marine of exceptional judgment who had shown his courage in battle. Easy Company, in turn, was part of the Second Battalion, commanded by Colonel Chandler Johnson, another tough-minded leader. The Second was assigned to the Twenty-eighth Regiment, commanded by Colonel Harry "the Horse" Liversedge. The Horse, like Johnson and Severance below him, was pure Marine—focused and dedicated.

The new fighting force soon received the honor of its own special name: Spearhead. Its insignia was a scarlet shield and gold *V*, pierced by a spearhead of blue. The name was a salute to the division's intended role in the grim island battles that lay ahead. Yet no one knew which island would be attacked first. That was a closely held secret.

The six flag raisers and the rest of the men of Easy Company went through intense and thorough training. Every Marine, regardless of his ultimate role in combat, was trained with the MI rifle.

By April all units were drilling in the field, training with live ammo, crawling, running, doing the same tasks over and over until they were done perfectly. As spring gave way to summer the boys began the first stages of amphibious training: conditioning these thousands of hard-bodied marksmen and technical specialists to move over the sides of troop transports into small landing vehicles—LVTs—and then to climb from these into shallow water, and then onto enemy beaches, all under intense hostile fire.

It was during these final phases of training that a distinguished visitor began to appear at Camp Pendleton. Many of the troops caught sight of him at a distance: a figure wrapped in a dark cape, sitting in a canvas chair beside an enormous black limousine.

In their midst, watching them train, conferring with their generals, was the legendary president whose "fireside chats" had kept some of these boys spellbound beside the radio only a few years before. By his presence alone, it was as if Franklin Delano Roosevelt was personally giving his blessing to the still secret mission of the Fifth Division of the United States Marines.

Throughout the six months at Pendleton all of Spearhead's boys, veterans and new Marines alike, sensed a new climate of respect from their officers. They were no longer mere recruits now; they were certified leathernecks. A year after their first action, the boys of Spearhead were already a brotherhood. *Semper fidelis*—"always faithful"—became as descriptive a phrase for these Marines as "death before dishonor."

My father typified this brotherhood. As the senior Navy corpsman of Easy Company, Doc had connections with the other five flag raisers. Though technically assigned to the Third Platoon, in practice he supervised the seven other corpsmen in the company; he would see to the needs of the entire company in combat. In this way, Second Platoon members Mike, Harlon, Ira, Franklin, and Rene came to see Doc not only as a potential lifesaver, but as an integral part of their daily lives.

Through all the rigorous days of training, my father was a calm center, a steadying influence on all the Easy Company boys around him, just as the famous photograph showed him: there in the midst of things, lending a hand. At twenty he was already regarded as the "old man" among the corpsmen. He went out of his way to help anyone who needed a favor. His kindness became his trademark.

It was at Camp Pendleton that my father met the young man who would become his best buddy in the service, and perhaps a key to his lifelong silence on the subject of his World War II experiences: Ralph "Iggy" Ignatowski. The name was nearly bigger than the boy who bore it. Like Doc, Iggy was a Wisconsin product, a baseball-and-bicycle kid, and the youngest of nine children in a close-knit Milwaukee family with strong European Catholic ties.

Like Rene Gagnon, Iggy was young, almost unthinkably

young, to be in combat training: He was seventeen during the advanced training at Pendleton, eighteen when Iwo Jima was assaulted. Like Franklin Sousley, he seemed to lack the temperament of a warrior; he was a sunny jokester, a warmhearted family boy. But there was steel beneath that surface gentleness: Iggy had been determined to enlist in the Marines upon graduation from high school.

At Pendleton Doc and Iggy gravitated toward each other and quickly teamed up under the Marines' buddy system. Although the Marines warned their troops against forging too many friendships—knowing that combat would rip huge, heartbreaking holes in these networks—the Corps recommended that each man identify one other who would be his close ally in combat, his eyes and ears—and possibly the comforter of his parents. On this the two Wisconsin boys formed their bond.

Mike Strank was widely regarded as having one of the regiment's best squads, which included Harlon, Ira, and Franklin. Mike functioned on many different levels with many different men: as confidant, advisor, or conscience.

For Ira Hayes, he was all three. Ira Hayes's close friends made up a very narrow circle—Mike, Franklin, Harlon, and Doc were among its most intimate—and those outside that circle, such as Rene Gagnon, were mostly greeted with silence. Ira respected Mike and Harlon because they, like him, were veterans tested by combat. But his respect for Mike bordered on adulation. Ira would talk to the Czech-born sergeant intimately and intelligently, as he would to no one else.

Anyone not in Ira's inner circle could only guess at his

thoughts —except for Kenneth Milstead, who heard Ira's pain in the dead of the night. "I would have guard duty with Ira often. We'd be sitting there alone guarding some gate, no one around, just pitch black. Ira was always depressed. Over and over he'd repeat, 'I have nothing to go back to. There's nothing waiting for me at home when I get back.' "

Perhaps Ira's unlikeliest pal was Franklin Sousley. Franklin arrived at Camp Pendleton as a good ol' boy of eighteen, rawboned, his rust-colored hair uncombed. He stood six feet now, all of it muscle and bone. But the jokey sweetness was still intact: Franklin was as lighthearted as Ira was dour. He was one of the few who could make Ira (and nearly anyone else at Pendleton) laugh.

Few seemed to have much fondness for Rene Gagnon. One of the youngest and most sheltered of the Marines in the company, Rene was socially awkward around men. His comrades in arms seemed to recoil from the slight, callow nineteen-year-old almost by reflex. The memories of him among the guys of Easy Company are almost withering: "He seemed like a guy who didn't want his body hurt." "I didn't like him from the moment I met him." "He was looking for the easy way out."

It fell to Mike to try to turn Rene around. He rode the boy hard, pointing out every screwup, making him the butt of his jokes and ridicule, until Captain Severance decided that Rene could never quite fit in and reassigned him as a runner, a messenger reporting to headquarters. It wasn't cruelty that motivated Mike; it was the larger goal of saving lives. And with the transfer, Rene remained a member of the company. The other Marines were relieved, and Rene saw no problem in it. "I figured it would be a pretty good deal, getting the jeep and running errands for headquarters," he later said.

Harlon Block's time at Pendleton was a mix of diligent training and quiet contemplation. Training was seemingly effortless for him, and there were few who could match his stamina and strength. But in private Harlon continued to wrestle with his thoughts, many of them dark ones. No doubt he could hear Belle's voice in his head, admonishing him to uphold his Seventh-Day Adventist beliefs. That was impossible now—he had already been through Bougainville and now was being trained to kill again—but he may well have felt a conflict. And there was his growing belief that whatever the next mission was, he would not return home alive.

In their half year at Camp Pendleton the Marines of the Fifth Division had survived biting insects, rain, cold, hot sun, bad food, and rattlesnakes; they had learned all that the officers and facilities at the surreal city of men could teach them. Now it was time to board ship and sail off into the ocean, toward another training facility at a destination as yet unnamed, and learn some more.

On September 19—Franklin's birthday, as it happened—the Marines left San Diego harbor in troopships. Many of them would never see their American homeland again. But all of them would get a glimpse of paradise before the firestorm to come.

Paradise—Hawaii—looked lush and green and inviting from the rails of the ships dropping anchor in Hilo Bay. Few boys from the American heartland had ever seen anything quite so exotic.

Their arrival, however, burst the illusion and brought them back to earth—dusty, hardscrabble earth. Spearhead's destination was yet another training facility: Camp Tarawa.

Here, in the final four months before the great armada departed for its still top-secret destination—for the Japanese island known only as X—the Marines would fine-tune the specialized skills they would need for their great challenge. They would learn how to disembark, take the beach, turn left, and cut off the mountain.

The word *disembark* hardly suggests the stomach-wrenching process of climbing down cargo nets pitched over the sides of the great transport ships—every step encumbered by heavy packs—and securing a seat in one of the smaller landing craft. The young men were forced to make their descent as the huge transports bobbed and yawed in the turbulent waves. Some lost their footing and plunged into the water, others found themselves jammed against the ships by a sudden collision of hull against hull.

While the boys trained, their colonels and generals plotted strategy according to specific orders they had received from Washington. The officers dissected this strategy inside a forbidding-looking wooden structure near division headquarters at Camp Tarawa—a building that bore the deceptively innocuous name of "conference center."

The conference center's windows were blacked out, its shut doors sealed with double locks, its premises cordoned off with barbed wire and the constant presence of armed MPs. No one could enter the conference center without a special pass.

It was inside this dark building that a small training staff was told in November of 1944 that island X was Iwo Jima.

My father passed his days at Camp Tarawa attending to his duties and thinking of home. From what his friends recalled of him, he clung to his characteristic serenity and exceptional focus.

A dream burned in my father's heart—a clear, simple dream of returning to Wisconsin and opening his own funeral home—even as a firestorm on earth brewed on the other side of the ocean. No doubt that dream was one of the things that kept him alive.

His friend Robert Lane remembered Doc's tranquility in those days. "He was more mature than most guys," Lane said. "He used to tell me how he handled people who were suffering the loss of a loved one. He had already done that often in his life, in the funeral business."

The Fifth Division's days at Camp Tarawa were soon to end. December 1944 was the last Christmas for too many young boys. Then off for the forty-day sail to Iwo Jima. The boys of Spearhead had been expertly trained for ten months. They were proficient in the techniques of war. But more important, they were a team, ready to fight for one another. These boys were bonded by feelings as strong or stronger than they would have for any other humans in their life.

SIX

Armada

Don't worry about me, Momma. I'll be OK.
—From the last letter of an Iwo Jima–bound Marine

There were no cheering crowds to see Mike, Harlon, Ira, Doc, Rene, and Franklin off as they departed Camp Tarawa. To maintain military secrecy they journeyed in the dead of night.

Their destination was island X. That was all they knew. For the Marines fighting America's war in the Pacific, it was a familiar pattern: months of training, the invasion of an island no one had ever heard of, followed by more training and another invasion.

After a brief furlough at Pearl Harbor, the boys set sail on the USS *Missoula*, part of a convoy that was seventy miles long at sea. Two days out of Honolulu the identity of island X was revealed to the troops. This would not be a mere battle. It was to be a cultural collision on an almost mythic scale, and the results would alter the fates of both East and West for the rest of the century.

This giant fleet of American warships—a modern armada—churned across the ocean day and night. The four-thousand-mile journey took three weeks. On the *Missoula*, as on the other ships, accommodations were less than comfortable. There were only small spaces on the boat to mingle, so most of the men had to remain in their bunks, along with their pack, rifle, and helmet. The *Missoula* carried all of Easy Company amid its fifteen hundred troops. By the time this fleet converged with a second one, hurrying northward from down near Australia, the total number of ships would exceed eight hundred. All of these ships, all of these men—one hundred thousand, including Navy support personnel and Coast Guard units—would converge on an eight-mile-square island six hundred miles south of Tokyo.

Some troops in World War II would have the honor of liberating Paris, others Manila. Easy Company had been assigned an ugly hunk of slag in the ocean, nearly barren of trees or grass. The vanquishing of Iwo Jima was deemed imperative. Home to a fleet of Japanese warplanes and artillery batteries, two airstrips, and a radar station, the enemy had been shooting down too many U.S. planes on bombing runs from Saipan and Tinian to the Japanese mainland. Only a full-bodied assault by Navy and Marine forces could put the Japanese island out of commission.

Bulging at its northeast plateau, tapering down to Mount Suribachi at its southwestern tip, Iwo Jima resembles an upside-down pear with Suribachi at its stem. Pilots who photograph the island from above have another metaphor: They think the island resembles a charred pork chop.

Mount Suribachi is an extinct volcano, and the lava flow from its eruptions over thousands of years formed the rest of the island. As maps were being unfurled on ships throughout the armada, it was clear that the only practical landing beach began at Suribachi's base and extended two miles along the eastern shore. I can only imagine what the flag raisers thought as they bent over these secret maps. They must surely have focused on their landing beach, stamped "Green Beach." And they would have seen the designation the mapmakers had given Suribachi: "Hot Rocks."

The Marine invasion plan was direct and to the point. Harry the Horse's Twenty-eighth Regiment, with Easy Company among it, would land closest to Hot Rocks. They were part of the group that would string out in a ribbon of men across the narrow neck of the island, cutting Mount Suribachi off from the rest of the island. Then they'd pivot left to take the volcano.

The surface of Iwo Jima was rendered white on the map. But the white was almost totally obscured by little black dots. These black dots represented the armaments that would fire at them as they struggled up Green Beach and raced inland in the shadow of Hot Rocks. Just about every type of defense available in 1945 was represented by those black dots. All were identified by the key on the map: coastal defense guns, dual-mount dual-purpose guns, covered artillery emplacements, rifle pits, foxholes, antitank guns, machine guns, blockhouses, pillboxes, and earth-covered structures.

Another frightening aspect of the coming battle stuck in the back of many boys' minds. Unlike Tarawa or Bougainville, the Japanese considered Iwo Jima as homeland. In Shinto mythology, the island was part of the creation that burst forth from

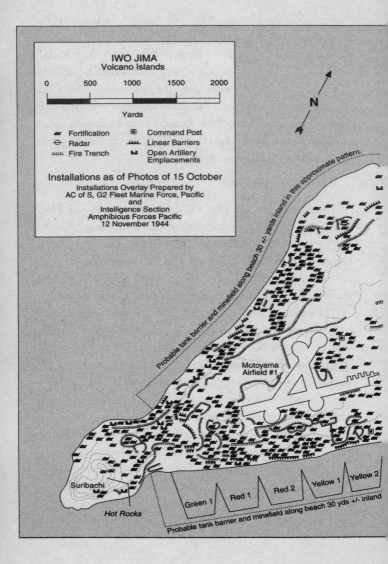

IWO JIMA
Volcano Islands

0   500   1000   1500   2000

Yards

Fortification   Command Post
Radar   Linear Barriers
Fire Trench   Open Artillery Emplacements

Installations as of Photos of 15 October

Installations Overlay Prepared by
AC of S, G2 Fleet Marine Force, Pacific
and
Intelligence Section
Amphibious Forces Pacific
12 November 1944

N

Probable tank barrier and minefield along beach 30 +/- yards inland in this approximate pattern.

Motoyama Airfield #1

Suribachi

Hot Rocks

Green 1   Red 1   Red 2   Yellow 1   Yellow 2

Probable tank barrier and minefield along beach 30 yds +/- inland

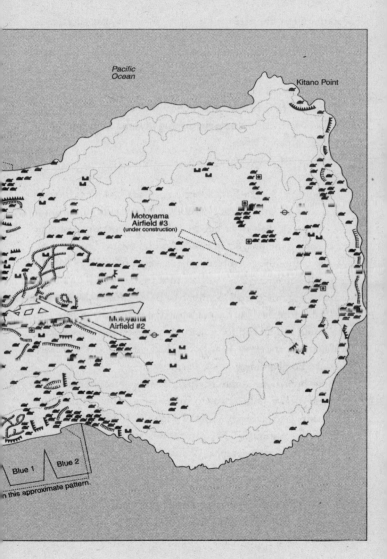

Mount Fuji at the dawn of history. Modern-day governance honored that tradition: The mayor of Tokyo, only 650 miles away, was also the mayor of Iwo Jima. The island was part of a sacred realm that had not been desecrated by an invader's foot for four thousand years.

As far as the Japanese were concerned, Easy Company and the other Marines would be attempting nothing less than the invasion of imperial Japan.

By February 11 the Fifth Division armada had rendezvoused with the Third and Fourth Divisions at Saipan. Filling the horizon were more than eight hundred ships, pausing one last time before sailing the final seven hundred miles to Iwo Jima.

Long before the assembled armada sailed on its final leg, the Army Air Force was doing its part to soften up Iwo Jima for the invasion. Beginning on December 8, B-29 Superfortresses and B-24 Liberators had been pummeling the island mercilessly. Iwo Jima would be bombed for seventy-two consecutive days, setting the record as the most heavily bombed target and the longest sustained bombardment in the Pacific war.

Some hoped the unprecedented bombing would make the conquest of Iwo Jima a two- to three-day job. But on the command ship USS *Eldorado*, General Howlin' Mad Smith shared none of this optimism. The general was studying the latest air reconnaissance photographs. While it was clear that every square inch of the island had been bombed, enemy defenses were actually growing. Comparative aerial photos showed there had been 450 major defensive installations when the bombing began. Now there were more than 750.

The day the invaders sailed from Saipan, General Tadamichi
Kuribayashi, in charge of all Japanese troops on Iwo Jima, ordered his men to take their battle stations. He had no
expectation that he could win the battle. He knew the Americans
would throw overwhelming arms and numbers of men at him.
But he also knew Tarawa and Bougainville had aroused concern
in America about unacceptable losses. Now Kuribayashi wanted
to make Iwo Jima so costly in American lives that the leaders in
Washington would blanch at the prospect of a later invasion of
the Japanese home islands and instead would want to negotiate a
peace with Japan. To this end, Kuribayashi had instructed his
men to "kill ten Americans before you die."

His *issen gorin*, or drafted soldiers, had long ago written the final letters that would be delivered to their families back home.
To his own wife Kuribayashi had written, "Do not expect my
return."

The Japanese army used the most ruthless tactics of any
combatant in World War II. Their practice of "no surrender"
meant they were unpredictable, as they fought far beyond the
limits of most Westerners. If surrounded, a German would surrender; a Japanese would fight on. If wounded and disabled, an
Englishman would allow himself to be taken prisoner; a Japanese would wait and blow himself and his captor up with a
grenade.

Because the Japanese fought by different rules, the Marines
changed some of theirs. I think of Doc, my twenty-one-year-
old father-to-be, on that LVT heading to the shore of Iwo
Jima. He's Doc to everyone, a Navy corpsman. In the European

theater my dad would have worn a red cross on his helmet and expected the Germans to spare him as a noncombatant. And he would have been unarmed, according to the Geneva Convention. But the Pacific theater was different. The Japanese targeted corpsmen to prevent them from helping wounded Americans. So Doc was dressed like any other Marine—there was no red cross on his helmet—and he knew how to use the .45-caliber pistol that he carried.

Perhaps the biggest fear of the boys was fear of the unknown. How many troops would be on Iwo Jima? Would air and naval bombardment eliminate most? How long would the land engagement take? American intelligence analysts had many aerial photographs of Iwo Jima, but they rarely revealed a Japanese soldier. Because of the island's lack of drinking water, they concluded only thirteen thousand troops could be there. They were off by 40 percent—in reality there were twenty-two thousand Japanese, all of whom knew exactly where the invaders would arrive. Only two miles of beach on the entire perimeter were suitable for an assault. All the Marines would have to go through this narrow funnel under the deadly gaze of Mount Suribachi.

General Kuribayashi was determined to cause as many casualties as possible over the longest possible time. He concluded that he would fortify the interior of the island and make it a killing field. He had sifted the coarse volcanic beach sand through his fingers and knew the Americans and their tanks and artillery would bog down on the beaches. He would wait until the beach was crowded with bodies and machines. Then his troops would open fire from their positions above the beach. Hardly a Japanese bullet could miss.

And any American who made it off the beach would enter a frightening no-man's-land with the enemy underground, unseen. Long before the inevitable invasion, Kuribayashi had set about building the most ingenious fortress in the history of warfare. With the help of Japanese mining engineers, the general created a subterranean cave system connected by tunnels. The caves were thirty to fifty feet deep and had ventilation, stairways, and passageways. Lighting ranged from electricity to fuel lamps and candles. There was space for storing ammunition, food and water, and other supplies. The caverns had multiple entrances and exits to avoid entrapment. Underground housing, meeting rooms, communications centers, and even hospitals complete with surgical equipment and operating tables took shape. One hospital could treat four hundred men on stone beds carved into the rock walls.

By the fall of 1944 a city of twenty-two thousand men was functioning below the surface of the earth. General Kuribayashi would direct the battle from his command center, a bombproof capsule that was seventy-five feet underground. The black dots that the Americans had observed on their battle maps were only the surface openings of this elaborate underground system: the tip of the iceberg, the spout of the submerged whale. By the time General Kuribayashi was finished and waited for the United States invasion, Iwo Jima was far and away the most heavily fortified island of World War II.

The invasion of Iwo Jima was primarily a Navy operation. General Smith's Marines, were, in effect, the Navy's land troops. Smith requested a full ten days of heavy shelling of the island before the Marines rushed ashore. When the Navy admirals responded that their battleships would only provide three days of bombardment "due to limitations on the availability of ships, difficulties of ammunition replacement, and the loss of surprise," General Smith was, well, howling mad.

What was "loss of surprise"? Smith knew that the Japanese couldn't be surprised after seventy days of bombing by planes and the sure knowledge of an armada of 880 ships sailing toward them. He was convinced that replaceable ammunition could be found to save irreplaceable lives. But the key was the phrase "the availability of ships."

Was not the capture of Iwo Jima the main Allied objective in the Pacific? The Navy's admirals, however, were eager to grab headlines and show that they, too—not only the Army Air Force—could shell Japan. Ships were being diverted to the high-profile mission of bombing the enemy's homeland.

A furious Smith made increasingly desperate pleas for more bombardment—nine days, then seven, until he was down to four, just one more day than the Navy had arbitrarily assigned. All his requests were denied. Then the Navy added a final insult: There would be even fewer ships available for the shelling of Iwo Jima than agreed upon. Additional ships were needed for the bombing of Japan's main islands.

Then things got even worse. The Navy shelling of Iwo Jima was scheduled for February 16, 17, and 18, but due to weather and technical complications, only February 17 saw a complete day of bombardment.

Smith would be forever bitter about the Navy's almost indifferent posture to the invasion. "If the Marines had received better cooperation from the Navy," he wrote after the war, "our casualties would have been lower."

The evening of D day minus one, February 18, a date that nine years later would become my birthday, my father and the assault troops waited quietly aboard their ships. Each boy was lost in his private thoughts. Everybody's confidence must have been shaken when that night Tokyo Rose—the official radio voice and propaganda arm of the Japanese military—in perfect English named many of the U.S. ships and a number of the Marine units.

General Kuribayashi was in his personal quarters seventy-five feet below the surface of the earth. The dim candlelight illuminated the "Courageous Battle Vow" posted on the wall, as he had ordered it posted by everyone on the island. In part it read:

> *We are here to defend this island to the limit of our strength. . . .*
> *We cannot allow ourselves to be captured by the enemy. . . . No*
> *man must die until he has killed at least ten Americans. We will harass*
> *the enemy with guerrilla actions until the last of us has perished. Long*
> *live the Emperor!*

SEVEN

D Day

*Life was never regular again. We were changed from the
day we put our feet in that sand.*

—Private Tex Stanton, Second Platoon, Easy Company

The sun rose pink. The sky turned blue and clear. On the horizon, Iwo Jima lay wreathed in smoke.

The date was February 19, 1945.

The cooks on the transport ships had provided a gourmet breakfast for the young men about to go into battle: steak and eggs. Hours later, more than seventy thousand Marines—the Third, Fourth, and Fifth Divisions—massed for the invasion. For the boys of Easy Company, their year of special training at Camp Pendleton and Camp Tarawa had transformed them into a team, a band of brothers, prepared to pay any price for one another. At seven o'clock that morning the boys of Easy Company walked down the metal steps of LST-481 and into the holds of their assigned amphibious tractors, about twenty to a boat. Loaded with men, the first waves of amphibious landing craft began surging toward the island at full throttle, kicking up white foam in their wake. Behind and above them was an overwhelming American force: in the sea, the armada at anchor, vessels stretching away from shore for ten miles; in the air, flights of Navy Hellcats swooping low to strafe Mount Suribachi, reshaping its contours with their firepower.

In those final moments before the first landing, many in the boats could still convince themselves that this was going to be no sweat. Wasn't the island being blown to bits even as the amtracs churned toward shore? No one could have known about the extensive caves and tunnels of the *issen gorin* or been aware that the bombardment had not even affected them. The battle for Iwo Jima would quickly turn into a primitive contest of gladiators: Japanese gladiators fighting from caves and tunnels and American gladiators aboveground, exposed on all sides, using napalm, a kind of jellied gasoline, to burn their opponents out of their hiding places. All of this on an island five and a half miles long and two miles wide. A car driving sixty miles an hour could cover its length in five and a half minutes. For the slogging, fighting, dying Marines, it would take more than a month.

The naval bombardment ceased precisely at 8:57 A.M. Five minutes later, at 9:02, armored tractors, each mounted with a 75mm cannon, lumbered from the waves onto the soft black sands of Iwo Jima. At 9:05 the first troop-carrying amtracs landed, and behind them came hundreds more. Easy Company rolled in on the twelfth wave at 9:55 A.M. Easy was part of Harry the Horse's Twenty-eighth Regiment, whose special mission was to land on Green Beach One—the stretch nearest Mount Suribachi, which was just four hundred yards away, on

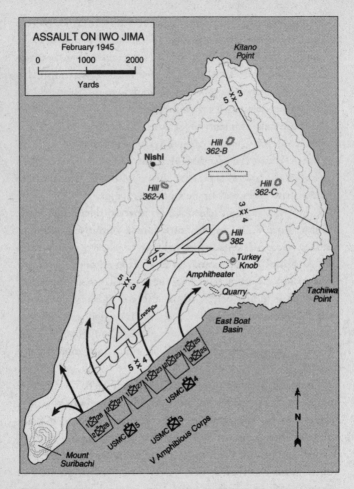

the left—and then form a ribbon of men across the narrow neck of the island, isolating the fortified mountain and ultimately capturing it. And so the great funneling from wide ocean to narrow beach had begun: hordes of wet, equipment-burdened boys slogging from the water, forming a tightly packed mass on the two-mile strip of beach.

The boys squinted upward at their assigned routes and the ugly, stunted mountain beyond. The beach slanted upward from a point some thirty yards from the edge of the surf; it rose in three terraces, each about eight feet high and sixteen feet apart. The boys would have to climb not on hard white sand but on soft black volcanic ash that gave way and made each upward step a lingering effort.

When the first wave of Marines and armored vehicles hit the shores, the vehicles bogged down immediately in the soft sand, just as General Kuribayashi had hoped. The troops moved around their stalled vehicles and began their cautious climb, un-shielded, up the terraces.

It was quiet at first. The false calm was part of General Kuribayashi's radical strategy: to hold off from firing at once and wait until the funneling attackers had filled the beach.

Easy Company had been ashore some twenty minutes and were in their assembly area when the first Japanese fire was heard. Smoke and earsplitting noise suddenly filled the universe. The almost unnoticed blockhouses on the flat ground facing the ocean began raking the exposed troops with machine-gun bullets. The Americans became targets in a shooting gallery.

The real firestorm erupted from the mountain, from Suri-bachi: mortars, heavy artillery shells, and machine-gun rounds ripped into the stunned Americans. Two thousand hidden Japanese were gunning them down with everything from rifles to coastal defense guns.

There was no protection. Suddenly the mortars and bullets began tearing in from all over the island: General Kuribayashi had designed an elaborate cross fire from other units to the north. Entire platoons were engulfed in fireballs. Boys clawed frantically at the soft ash, trying to dig holes, but the ash filled in each swipe of the hand or shovel. Heavy rounds sent jeeps and armored tractors spinning into the air in fragments.

"I was watching an amtrac to the side of us as we went in," Easy Company's Robert Leader remembers. "Then there was this enormous blast and it disappeared. . . . Everything just vaporized."

In the same boat with Leader was Doc Bradley. The boys on the beach scrambled forward. It was like climbing in talcum powder, said one. Like a bin of wheat. Like deep snow.

Advancing tanks crushed those of the wounded who could not get out of the way. Others, unwounded, were shoved to their deaths by those behind them. "More and more boats kept landing with more guys coming onto the beach," remembered one Marine. "You had to just push the guy in front of you. It was like pushing him to his death."

The shock of actual combat triggered bizarre thoughts and behavior. Some Marines dropped into a deep, terror-induced sleep amid the carnage and had to be kicked awake by their officers. It became an outright slaughter. As far as the Japanese were concerned, the battle plan was going according to script. The Americans were falling right into their hands.

Total destruction seemed possible in the hideous first minutes of the landing. Radio transmissions back to command quarters aboard the ships were ominous: "Taking heavy casualties and can't move for the moment!" "Mortars killing us!"

"Need tank support fast to move anywhere!" "Machine-gun and artillery fire heaviest ever seen!"

But it was even worse than what the transmissions indicated. No one was out of danger. A five-foot-five Associated Press photographer named Joe Rosenthal, landing with the Fourth Division, ran for his life through the hail of bullets. Later he would declare that "not getting hit was like running through rain and not getting wet."

The first wave of Easy Company Marines, caught on the terraces in their heavy packs, scrambled for survival. "Like climbing a waterfall," one remembered. Jerry Smith pressed himself as close to the ground as he could and felt bullets rip through his backpack. "Even the socks in my pack had bullet holes in them," he recalls. The volcanic ash slowed progress, but in another sense it saved lives: the ash absorbed many of the mortar rounds and shrapnel, muffling explosions and sucking in the lethal fragments.

Lieutenant Ed Pennel's Second Platoon nearly lost its way in these early moments of deafening chaos. The unit, with Mike as a squad leader and Harlon, Franklin, and Ira in the ranks, landed far off course, north of Green Beach. "I was a very scared son-of-a-gun," Ira Hayes wrote later. "Our boat hit solid ground and the ramp went down. I jumped clear of the ramp. About three yards away lay a dead Marine right on the water's edge, shot in the head. He hadn't begun to fight. My stomach turned flip-flops."

Somehow the Marines kept advancing. Somehow discipline held. Somehow valor overcame terror and scared young men under sheets of deadly fire kept on doing the basic, gritty tasks that they'd practiced over and over in training.

The calming presence of veterans in their midst was one factor in their favor. Mike Strank, true to form, never lost his composure. In the opening moments of Japanese mortar fire, Lloyd Thompson looked up and could not believe what he saw: "There was Mike, sitting upright, emptying the sand out of his boots. Just as if nothing was happening."

Having made his point of remaining focused, Mike was soon shepherding his boys across the sands to their rendezvous with Dave Severance's main unit. Joe Rodriguez remembers him dashing back and forth among his squad members, cautioning them to spread out: "Don't bunch up! Don't be like a bunch of bananas!"

It was gestures such as Mike's—probably hundreds of them, most lost to history—that enabled the Americans to withstand the maelstrom of hidden firepower, and even to begin inflicting damage of their own.

But damage against what? That was the constant question at Iwo Jima. There were no targets. The gunners were invisible, protected, creatures of the underworld.

Even when they claimed a casualty, the Marines could rarely see it: The Japanese quickly pulled their dead and wounded back inside the caves and blockhouses. Thus there was little evidence of the invasion's impact. In the days that followed, observers of the battle in spotter planes high above the action would remark that it looked as though the Marines were fighting the island itself.

And yet the Americans did inflict damage that brutal first morning, using the same excruciating means by which they would continue to inflict it for thirty-six days, until all the twenty-two thousand defenders were wiped out: by exposing themselves to fire, charging the fortified blockhouses and cave entrances, and shooting or incinerating their tormentors at close range.

An early mistake in the invasion was to assume that a source of enemy fire, once extinguished, was permanently dead. General Kuribayashi's vast tunneling system ensured that many Marines were shot as they moved past a "neutralized" nest that had been quickly repopulated from below the ground.

Tangible progress was achieved in the opening hour and a half of combat. By 10:35 A.M. a small group of men from the first assault waves—Company A of the Twenty-eighth Regiment—had survived a near-suicidal, seven-hundred-yard dash across the island to the western beach. Already Suribachi was cut off from the rest of the island.

Meanwhile, other brave boys were doing grunt work near the shoreline, work that would get the mechanized part of the assault in motion. Oblivious to the storm of lead and steel, some bent down and shoved wire mats under the treads of mired tanks; others calmly climbed into bulldozers to begin roughing out the semblance of a road system. These were the instincts of training and courage that took hold as the first shock of battle wore off. Their courage was fueled by a fierce kind of love and devotion.

Father Paul Bradley, a priest, went in on the third wave. "I was young," he recalled later, "and didn't think about the danger to me. And I was too busy crawling from dying man to dying man. It was always, 'Father, over here!' Once I was kneeling in the sand administering to a guy who had been hit. There was a loud thud. His eyes closed. He'd been hit again and was dead. 'Father, over here!' someone called. I went on to the next one."

In the midst of all this carnage and confusion was my father—my father with his corpsman's pouch, called a "unit 3," slung over his shoulder. The Japanese on Iwo Jima had been trained to look for corpsmen by identifying their telltale medical pouch—and shoot them on the spot. Without a corpsman to save the wounded, the Japanese knew, their kill ratio would be much higher. My dad was aware he was a target, but that knowledge didn't keep him from doing his job. Thurman Fogarty, eighteen then, remembered the "welter of blood" that engulfed the Navy doctors and corpsmen as soon as they landed. Fogarty himself was buffeted by the concussions of the big shells coming in and going out, like powerful gusts of wind. After just a few minutes he fell to the beach and scraped out as much of an indentation as he could. Doc Bradley was crouched next to him, attending to a small wound in his own leg.

"I happened to look to my left and saw that the Marine next to me had his arm almost blown off," Fogarty said. "It was just dangling from his shoulder. I pointed this out to Doc. He looked up from his own wounds and rolled across my legs to attend the injured Marine. The guy was conscious. Doc calmly put a tourniquet on the stump of the arm and told the guy to hold it. Then he shot him full of morphine and tied the dangling arm to the stump. And then pointed him toward the aid station."

John Fredatovich, also eighteen, would become Easy's first

casualty and had need of Doc Bradley nearly as soon as he broke from the water. He recalled it vividly: "I heard the mortar, then I felt a cold chill, the shock to my nervous system as the shrapnel penetrated my arm and leg. . . . Doc came over. . . . He was very forceful and took charge. He gave me blood transfusions as I went in and out of consciousness. Then four Marines carried me away to a place on the beach for evacuation."

The place where Fredatovich lay offered no protection from the firestorm. Every inch of the beach was an active target. Fredatovich saw a boatload of Marines lifted out of the water in a giant flash and exploded into nothingness. He saw other wounded boys on their stretchers get blown to pieces. The sight that returned to the future teacher most often in memory, however, was a strikingly unlikely one: a glimpse of Harlon Block as Harlon ran past him toward the action.

"I called up to him; I said hi," Fredatovich remembered, "but he just ran on by. It was the look in his eyes that startled me. He had a glazed, blank look. It was as if memories were coming back to him from past experiences. This surprised me. I later studied psychology and I realized that those dilated pupils meant he was shocked by something and was transfixed on some image from his past. It was as if the noise of the mortars transported him to a past memory."

By noon the heavy casualties continued but the threat of annihilation had vanished. Nine thousand troops were ashore, and more were on their way. The Marines were on Iwo Jima to stay.

Through the long afternoon the Americans held their positions and even advanced, despite the continuing nightmare of fighting an invisible enemy. The Japanese cross fire came from everywhere on the island; even the artillery near Kitano Point, nearly five miles to the north, was delivering shells in sheets.

Advancing vehicles were blown up by aircraft bombs embedded in the sand as tank mines. "Spider traps" and caves linked to the tunneling system were everywhere. They gave the defenders countless places from which to pop up, fire, disappear, and surface again. The difference between living and dying was sheer luck, many survivors said later. You were a target if you moved—and you were a target if you stayed in place.

And yet, as one Marine recalled, "We did what we were ordered to do. We worked our way across the center of that island with machine guns firing at us. We'd jump into a tank ditch for protection and then our leader would yell, 'Mine!' and we'd change direction. We'd blast pillboxes, secure them just like in training. But unlike in training they'd come alive again and fire at us from the rear. But we made it. . . . We got across the island."

Getting ashore proved more difficult as the day progressed— and not just because of the gunfire. Stacks of dead Marines and burned-out amtracs formed an almost impenetrable barrier in the ocean and on the beach. Nevertheless, eight battalions were onshore by the afternoon, as were the tank battalions of two divisions and elements of two artillery battalions.

Miraculously, by nightfall the beachhead was secured. As the sun set, the shoreline grew even more grotesquely clogged with human bodies: Each Marine returning for supplies from the front brought a dead or wounded man with him. Their groans could be heard up and down the shore as darkness set in. Uncounted numbers of them died there, blasted by shells as they lay on their stretchers, waiting to be evacuated to the hospital ships.

The first night on Iwo Jima brought its own special horrors. The leaders of Spearhead hardly rested. Colonel Harry Liversedge moved his command post two hundred yards nearer the front, to be ready for the next morning's assault on the mountain.

In the waters offshore, boats churned through the night, bringing in more of the living, taking away more of the dying. At the White House, President Roosevelt shuddered when told of the Americans' first day on Iwo Jima. "It was the first time in the war, through good news and bad, that anyone had seen the President gasp in horror." The first day's fighting had claimed more than half as many casualties as the entire Guadalcanal campaign: 566 men killed ashore and afloat, and 1,755 wounded.

The remaining troops lay as still as they could through the night. The falling parachute flares illuminated everything; the shadows darted and slid. Any shadow might be a Japanese soldier, crawling softly for the kill.

One surgeon had established an operating theater in what he'd thought was a safe area. With sandbags and tarp he'd fashioned a makeshift hospital. But as he tried to sleep that night, he heard what sounded like foreign voices below him. Was he dreaming? He dug his fingers into the soft ash and felt for evidence. His fingertips scraped something solid: the wooden roof of a reinforced cavern. The surgeon had built his hospital directly atop the enemy.

The first day of the battle of Iwo Jima had come to an end. There were thirty-five left to go.

EIGHT

D Day Plus One

It is good that war is so horrible,
or we might grow to like it.

—Robert E. Lee

Rain greeted the boys of Easy Company as they awoke and looked out at Suribachi's squat bulk on Tuesday, February 20. Rain and cold gusts would lash them for the next three days. The surf, mercifully calm during the invasion, had risen with the night winds; it roiled and slammed its ugly gray foam onto the beach in four-foot waves. Now the unloading of equipment would be hampered by more than enemy artillery, and the mood among the high command was grim.

From their position above the western beaches, Mike, Ira, Harlon, and the others could hear the mortar, rocket, and artillery fire from Japanese guns. The shells wiped out two casualty stations on the assault beach, killing many already wounded men.

The young Marines had spent the night braced for a banzai

charge—hordes of *issen gorin* rushing insanely through the darkness toward the bivouacked Americans. This had been routine in other Pacific island battles. Although terrifying, these charges at least exposed the Japanese soldiers to the Marines' gun sights; usually the attackers lost many more men than the defenders.

But no banzai attacks came, not yet. The enemy could afford to wait. The mortar and big artillery shells that rained down on the Americans that night did far more damage than any charging soldiers with bayonets could do.

The early light of dawn showed that the Twenty-eighth Regiment—Harry "the Horse" Liversedge's outfit—had established itself across the narrow neck of the island, isolating Suribachi just a few hundred yards to the south. Now the three thousand men of the Twenty-eighth would begin their dangerous advance southward toward the volcano, while the other thirty-three thousand Marines on the island would fight their way north toward the airfields and the high fortified ground on the northern rim.

Soon after sunrise Colonel Liversedge positioned his Second and Third Battalions to continue their assault on Mount Suribachi. Easy Company was not among these units. They were held in regimental reserve. Easy would retrace their steps of the day before, going eastward to position themselves in the Second Battalion area. There they would assume a backup position, from which they could be rushed into the front lines.

But first Navy carrier planes came out of the wet sky to slam Suribachi with rockets, bombs, and napalm blobs. At eight-thirty Harry the Horse gave the order to attack. As the Marines zigzagged their way through the rain toward Suribachi, shells from nearby U.S. destroyers blasted the mountain.

The bombardment had little impact on the subterranean enemy, and the advancing Marines were raked with heavy rifle fire. Captain Severance committed Easy's First Platoon to the attack early in the day. The platoon leader, Lieutenant George Stoddard, was wounded and evacuated. The ground assault gained less than seventy-five yards through the morning, and those yards were earned the old-fashioned way, with flamethrowers and handheld guns.

While the attack surged and then stalled, Easy Company, minus the First Platoon, continued to pick its way east, always with the mountain and its gunners looming not far away. And the beach was still hot. Unlike Normandy's beaches, which fell quiet after twenty-four hours, the Iwo Jima shoreline continued to absorb casualties for days. But up on the front lines American boys were avenging these losses with a fury. Some of the fiercest of these warriors were just kids, like Jacklyn Lucas. He'd fast-talked his way into the Marines at fourteen. Assigned to drive a truck in Hawaii, he stowed away on a transport out of Honolulu, surviving on food passed along to him by sympathetic leathernecks on board. He landed on Iwo Jima on D day without a weapon.

Now Jack Lucas, with a rifle he'd grabbed on the beach, and three comrades were crawling through a trench when eight Japanese sprang in front of them. Jack shot one of them through the head. As his rifle jammed, a grenade landed at his feet. He yelled a warning to the others and rammed the grenade into the soft ash. Immediately another grenade rolled in. Jack fell on both.

His comrades wiped out the remaining enemy and returned to Jack to collect the dog tags from his body. To their amazement, they found their buddy not only alive but conscious. Aboard a hospital ship, the doctors could scarcely believe it. Jack endured twenty-one reconstructive operations and at seventeen years old became the nation's youngest Medal of Honor awardee.

When I asked Jack, fifty-three years after the event, "Mr. Lucas, why did you jump on those grenades?" he did not hesitate with his answer: "To save my buddies."

In the midst of battle the Marines buried their dead. There were so many casualties that a bulldozer would carve out mass graves a hundred feet long by ten feet wide.

Chaplain Gage Hotaling could never forget the bleak enormousness of these mass burials: "We buried fifty at a time. . . . We didn't know if they were Jewish, Catholic or whatever, so we said a general committal: 'We commit you into the earth and the mercy of Almighty God.' I buried eighteen hundred boys."

The Second Battalion clawed its way some one hundred yards toward Suribachi. The winter sun, which had emerged from the clouds late in the day, had now sunk behind the mountain, and the Marines of Easy Company moved directly into its giant shadow. Many of the young boys were seized with the feeling that the mountain was looking at them; in fact, it was. Thousands of Japanese, barricaded under Suribachi's craggy surface, were watching the Americans' every move.

Over the Marines' heads rounds from tanks and offshore destroyers slammed into the mountain. Navy and Marine fighter planes angled in, plastering the steep flanks with napalm that burst in bright orange plumes and incinerated everything in its path. On the ground, under fire, my father prowled, the unit 3 pouch slung over his shoulder identifying him to the enemy as he kept searching for the wounded.

"Our sick bay was just a rifle in the ground," recalled Dr. James Wittmeier, the battalion surgeon. "Doc Bradley came in with another casualty, and since he had been out with the troops so much I ordered him to rotate to the back and take a breather. He was tired, but he refused to stop. He said, 'I don't want to leave my men. I want to stay with them.' Then he went back to the fighting."

By the end of this day, the Fourth and Fifth Divisions controlled only a mile and a half of the island. For this, the Fifth Division had suffered some fifteen hundred casualties, and the Fourth about two thousand. And still the Americans could not see their enemy; they saw little evidence that they had inflicted casualties. Psychologically it was as though they were shooting at—and getting shot by—phantoms.

As Suribachi's shadow lengthened into general darkness, Easy Company dug in for another cold, sleepless night. The fatigued boys knew what lay in store when the winter sun rose again. They knew that in the morning their battalion would have to assault the mountain.

Amid another night of star shells, flares, and searchlights forming eerie shadows on Suribachi's sides, a Japanese mortar shell hit a Marine ammunition dump on the beach. The explosion lit up the sky for an hour.

NINE

D Day Plus Two

Some people wonder all their lives if they've made a difference. The Marines don't have that problem.

—Ronald Reagan

In the darkened land of the phantoms, the fatigued Marines must have tried to sleep. For the ones who did, and for that matter those who didn't, the next day didn't begin with much promise: An unexpected winter storm was lashing in from the sea.

In the tense silence of first light, soaked, cold, and exhausted Marines gazed toward the primitive mass of rock that held their fates. Easy Company faced a long, lethal gauntlet on the volcano's northeastern side. Dave Severance's boys would have to rush across two hundred yards of open terrain toward the mountain's base, with very little cover of any kind.

The guns trained down on the two hundred yards between the Twenty-eighth Regiment and the mountain's base would soon make those yards the worst killing ground in the Pacific.

Not only were these two hundred yards barren of natural cover, but they lay in the teeth of ground fire from the thousands of Japanese popping up from their hiding spots belowground. In addition, on the mountain base stretched a welter of reinforced concrete pillboxes and infantry trenches. The firing ports of the pillboxes were angled so that the Japanese shooters could see one another and offer mutual support with their spewing machine guns.

The Marines' artillery quickly opened its own earth-shattering barrage. Hot "friendly" metal streaked low over the Marines' heads, splintering the rock on the side of the mountain. The boys on the perimeter ducked under the lethal salvos.

Toward the end of the artillery barrage, forty carrier planes screamed in low, drilling the mountain with rockets that exploded at an earsplitting pitch. Some of the bombs landed a football field's length away from the crouching Marines.

The planes pulled away. At exactly eight o'clock the boys braced themselves for the cry of "Attack!" But no order came. Colonel Liversedge had expected several tanks to arrive to cover the assault. When half an hour later none had arrived, the colonel, despite the absence of armor to cover the charging boys, could afford to wait no longer.

At eight-thirty a thin line of unprotected Americans rushed directly at the most fortified mountain in the history of the world. An electric current of pure terror pulsed across the regiment. The Marines could see that the tanks were not in the field. No tanks; no large bulky shapes to protect the boys against fire from the pillboxes as they ran. Nothing but bodies against bullets. A certainty of death filled the air. Then the heroes of the day began literally to stand up and be counted. One of the first was Lieutenant Keith Wells of Easy Company's Third Platoon. Wells did not tell his men to follow him. He simply got to his feet, waved his gun toward the mountain, and began running. "I just thought it was pure suicide," he later recalled.

Wells's example stirred the troops. Behind him, hundreds of scared boys stood, leveled their rifles, and advanced against the mountain. To the left of Wells's Third Platoon (with Doc Bradley) was Lieutenant Ed Pennel's Second Platoon (with Mike, Harlon, Ira, and Franklin) matching Wells's advance step by step.

The mountain exploded back at them. Mike, Harlon, Doc, Ira, and Franklin swept forward with the rest of Easy Company, in the vanguard of the attack. Immediately Japanese shells and bullets began cutting the Americans down. Amid the din the air was cut with kids' strangled voices calling, "Corpsman! Corpsman!"

Officers and enlisted men crumpled together under the hailstorm of steel. The slaughter continued though the morning. The Second Platoon, fighting hard on the left, found itself under a concentrated mortar barrage. Ira, Franklin, Harlon, and Mike zigzagged from one shell hole to another as they bore forward, looking for protection. Around them their friends were suffering and dying. Yet those who could kept advancing. Even as their casualties mounted at a rate that would have caused panic and retreat in nearly any other attacking force, these Marines remembered their training. Stoically they followed their assigned roles and kept moving forward as a team. In the midst of the carnage Doc Bradley ran through the chaos, doing what he could. He watched a Marine blunder into a flurry of machine-gun bursts and slump to the ground. Doc sprinted through thirty yards of cross fire to the wounded boy's side. As bullets whined and pinged around him, my father found the Marine losing blood at a life-threatening rate. Moving him was out of the question until the blood flow was stanched.

The Japanese gunfire danced all around him, but Doc stayed focused. He tied a plasma bottle to the kid's rifle and jammed it bayonet first into the ground. He moved his own body between the boy and the sheets of gunfire. Then, his upper body still erect and fully exposed, he administered first aid.

His buddies, watching him from their shell holes, were certain that he would be cut down at any moment. But Doc Bradley stayed where he was until he thought it was safe to move the boy. Then he raised a hand, signaling his comrades not to help but to stay low. My father stood into the merciless fusillade of bullets and pulled the wounded Marine back across the thirty yards to safety.

This action earned him his Navy Cross, an honor he never once mentioned to our family. It was one of the bravest things my father ever did, and it happened on one of the most valorous days in the history of a Corps known for valor.

Among the many heroes on the field was Lieutenant Keith Wells, the Third Platoon leader and the man who had stood up to inspire the first charge of the morning. Wells took a terrific hit in the early fighting. It happened as Easy, slogging toward the entrenched defenders, began taking fire not only from the front, but from the side.

Soon the company was pinned down by grenades and bullets from a blockhouse in its path. Worse, it came under a pinpoint barrage of close-in mortar fire. Two kids volunteered to go to the rear for more grenades; they were gunned down from the blockhouse. Then a shell burst near Lieutenant Wells, wounding him and four other men.

Wells suffered shrapnel wounds to his legs. Doc Bradley darted to his side, injected him with morphine, and told him to get to the rear. Wells would have none of it. His unit had begun the morning with forty-two men; twenty-five now remained. No one could be spared. The feeling had returned to his legs, and he decided to stay in the field, in command.

Lieutenant Wells's determination inspired his men. Flamethrowers Chuck Lindberg and Robert Goode arose with their deadly weapons and, ignoring the sheets of fire directed at them, stalked toward the pillbox and successfully destroyed it.

Soaked with blood, nearly immobilized by pain, Wells continued to direct the Third Platoon's attack through the late morning. But he grew weak. He fell once, dashing to elude gunfire, and reopened his wounds. Immediately Doc Bradley was at his side. Doc dosed him up with morphine again, meanwhile screaming, "Enough! Get out of here!"

Wells willed himself to stay in the field another half hour, directing assault groups and rallying his men. Finally, half delirious with pain and confident of victory, he turned his command over to Sergeant Ernest "Boots" Thomas and made for an aid station in the rear. He got there by crawling. He was awarded a Navy Cross.

The roar of tank treads now competed with the din of artillery all along the Marines' front as dozens of the tanks finally joined the front line. Shielded by the armored bulk, infantry-men could rush ever closer to pillboxes and bunkers without being exposed to fire. The inhabitants of those hovels—those who were not gunned down or scorched to death—began to flee toward the mountain. The Japanese first-line defenses were crumbling.

But the price of this victory remained high. Five of the flag raisers fought side by side, led by Lieutenants Wells and Pennel. Pennel himself was dashing from hole to hole when a shell landed between his legs and blew him a distance of thirty feet. His left heel was blown off, his right buttock and thigh gouged out, and his left shin pierced by shrapnel. An amphibious tractor tried to reach him. It hit a mine and blew up, killing the boys inside. Several hours later four Marines approached Pennel with a poncho. They rolled him onto it, each grabbed a corner, and they set off for the beach. A bullet wounded one of the carriers, and Pennel toppled heavily to the ground. The remaining three men dragged him to the beach. He lay there on a stretcher until darkness.

Half a century later Pennel recalled, "I felt exposed, like I was on a platform for all to see. Those flat-trajectory shells would skim straight in, making a roaring sound in the dark: *Foom! Foom! Foom!* Guys were being killed all around me. It was complete chaos."

Finally the lieutenant was loaded with some other wounded boys onto a pallet. An amtrac rushed them to an offshore hospital ship, where Pennel assumed he was at last out of harm's way. He assumed wrong. As a doctor examined him, a Japanese shell crashed onto the ship's deck and skittered into the fuel bunker. The doctor turned and, with Pennel, watched helplessly, doubtless wondering whether everyone nearby was about to be blown up. The shell turned out to be a dud.

As the rainy morning wore into afternoon and the fighting bogged down, the Marines continued to take casualties. Still the Americans kept fighting and advancing. By late in the bloody afternoon the conquest of the mountain seemed within the Marines' grasp.

But the Japanese—even as their ingenious fortifications crumbled or were scorched hollow—hadn't exhausted their own desperate resolve. As the Twenty-eighth continued to inch forward, Navy observation planes above the battle radioed that a swarm of Japanese had emerged from inside the mountain and was possibly forming for a banzai attack.

Within minutes American planes were swooping in to strafe the area. Their tremendous roar and the concussion of exploding rockets reverberated among the close-by Marines. The planes finally banked and vanished, and for a few moments the battlefield was silent.

It was Mike Strank, with the Second Platoon now on the left side of the line, who broke the stalemate. Rather then wait for the enemy to come to them, Mike decided he and his men would lead their own banzai charge at the pillboxes. Leaping to his feet, the bone-tired Czech immigrant led his battle-scarred Marines straight into the line of fire. The Japanese must have been stunned by the Americans' courage. To the right of the Second Platoon, the Third, commanded now by Boots Thomas, joined the charge.

Boots Thomas was the next hero to shine. With rough terrain

stalling the tanks some seventy-five yards to the rear, the twenty-year-old Floridian saw that his riddled unit was exposed once again. In the thick of battle he sprinted back through fire to the nearest tank and, still out in the open, directed its fire against the stubborn pillboxes. Then he dashed back to the front to exhort his men. A bit later he headed for the tanks again. He repeated this action several times.

Thomas's example paid off. The Third Platoon virtually annihilated the very enemy that had been massing for devastation of its own. As darkness on this triumphant, bloody day was setting in, Thomas himself identified the weak spot in the defensive line and personally led the breakthrough to Suribachi's steep flank. Boots was awarded the Navy Cross for his heroic actions.

Suribachi had not fallen, not quite, but victory for the Americans now seemed inevitable. The wet day ended with the Twenty-eighth Regiment poised in a vast semicircle around the battered volcano's base, gathering its strength for the finishing assault, expected to come the next morning.

For Easy Company it had been a day of grievous loss and historic valor. For this single day, the badly decimated unit would receive a Medal of Honor, four Navy Crosses, two Silver Stars, and numerous Purple Hearts—one of the most decorated engagements in the history of the United States Marine Corps. These honors were paid for in blood: Casualties for the day amounted to 30 percent of Easy's strength.

The Marines had paid for their advances across all fronts on the island with heavy losses. Official casualties for the battle now stood at 644 killed, 4,168 wounded, and 560 unaccounted for.

But the horrors of this day's fighting did not end with the

darkness. Just as dusk fell, an air raid signal alerted the ships offshore. From anyone on land looking out to sea, the thousands of tracers being fired were as beautiful as any Fourth of July. To the boys on board the task force ships, however, the sight was not quite so beautiful.

Cecil Gentry, a radio operator on the USS *Lawrence Taylor*, could not move when the order to hit the deck came from his captain. "I was transfixed," he said. "I just stood there. One plane flew right over my head. I could see the face of the Japanese pilot. You could see the fear of death on his face. His lips were pulled back over his teeth."

In a kamikaze dive, the pilot deliberately crashed into the USS *Bismarck Sea*, adjacent to the *Lawrence Taylor*. Four of the ship's own torpedoes detonated in the impact, and the great ship exploded in huge sheets of orange flame and rapidly sank. Over two hundred men were killed outright or lost at sea.

TEN

D Day Plus Three

It wasn't a matter of living or dying or fighting. It was a matter of helping your friends.

—Corpsman Robert DeGeus

On the fourth morning, the heaviest and coldest rains since D day lashed at the surviving Marines. The surf, whipped by twenty-knot winds, rolled in on nine-foot crests, and the rain made a black stew of the volcanic ash underfoot.

Easy Company prepared for a day of consolidation. Lieutenant Colonel Johnson ordered Severance to reorganize and re-supply his unit. The captain sent a patrol around the southern base of Suribachi to seek a linkup with the Third Battalion and to probe for enemy soldiers in the caves along the base of the volcano. American troops had converged on Suribachi, and the invaders' heavy equipment operated almost without resistance. Tanks, howitzers, and other big-bore weapons slammed Hot Rocks as though it were a target on a firing range. Battalion officers moved their command posts up to the brush line at the base of the slopes. Amphibious vehicles churned back and forth between the beaches and the front, bringing food and ammunition. Demolition specialists converged on pillboxes with a vengeance, relishing their payback for the slaughter those emplacements had dealt out.

Many of the enemy simply remained in the ground. Their muffled voices, and the sounds of their movement, added an eerie note to the mopping-up exercises. "We could hear them talking and moving right under our feet," one Marine recalled. "Right under what we'd thought was solid rock. We'd dig down and find a rafter. Then we'd lower explosives or pour in gasoline. Then they made a lot more noise."

The combat-weary Americans dealt in various ways with the memories of what they'd seen and done. Some talked to chaplains. Some lost themselves in their duties. For Ira Hayes, it was probably his edgy gallows humor that provided the shield against utter darkness. As Easy Company regathered itself at the base of Suribachi, Ira grew absorbed in shaping little mounds of earth with his hands. To others, the mounds looked like freshly dug graves, and in fact that seemed to be what Ira intended. When Franklin Sousley wandered past, Ira made a show of playing taps. Then he said to the Kentuckian: "This is just in case I'm not around when you get it."

By the end of the day the volcano known as Hot Rocks was surrounded, except for a four-hundred-yard gap on the western coast. Surrounded, but still dangerous: Some of the defenders who remained were determined killers.

As night fell, however, the Japanese themselves greatly reduced that danger through a highly uncharacteristic action: Many abandoned their positions. For all their vaunted loyalty to the emperor, and their general's orders that everyone fight to the death, some of the men, including officers, might have had different thoughts. Led by a lieutenant, 150 soldiers burst from the mountain in the middle of the night in a desperate race to join up with their forces to the north. Most were cut to pieces by Marines only too happy to deal at last with a visible enemy.

Only about twenty-five of the enemy made it through the gauntlet. When they arrived at the headquarters of the Japanese navy guard, their reception was not much better. The captain in charge, Samaji Inouye, accused their lieutenant of being a traitor and unsheathed his sword to behead the man. The lieutenant meekly bowed his neck, but a junior officer stopped him before he could swing his blade.

Captain Inouye then collapsed in uncontrollable sobs. "Suribachi's fallen," he moaned. "Suribachi's fallen."

Earlier that afternoon the American command had reached the same opinion, in a different frame of mind. Harry the Horse Liversedge received orders that the mountain be seized. Harry paid a visit to Colonel Johnson at his Second Battalion headquarters and issued a terse command: "Tomorrow we climb."

ELEVEN

The Flags

*I saw some guys struggling with a pole and I just jumped
in to lend them a hand. It's as simple as that.*

—Doc Bradley

Suribachi hulked above them still, before daybreak on the fifth
morning, this primitive serpent's head that had struck them down
in swaths. Amputated from the body, bombed, blasted, bayoneted,
burnt, Suribachi at last lay silent after four days of attack.

February 23, 1945, dawned cold and stormy, like the other
days on Iwo Jima, but by midmorning the rain had stopped and
the skies were clearing. The pugnacious Colonel Johnson called
for a scouting patrol to reconnoiter a path to the top. Following
the order, Sergeant Sherman B. Watson led a four-man patrol.
The small group was in for a surprise: The hostile fire that they
feared never materialized. Watson and his boys ventured all the
way to the volcano's lip and even risked a look into the crater,
finding a satisfying mass of wreckage, before scrabbling back
down to the base and reporting to Chandler Johnson.

Jack Bradley and family. *From left to right*: Kathryn (in the back),
Mary Ellen, Marge, Jack, Jim, and Cabbage.

Rene Gagnon.

Ira Hayes and his father, Jobe.

Franklin Sousley with his dog.

Mike Strank—First Communion.

Harlon Block and his brothers.
From left to right: Mel, Ed, Harlon, Larry, and Corky.

Harlon Block
in his USMC dress blues.

Rene Gagnon
in his USMC dress blues.

Jack Bradley
in his Navy dress blues.

Franklin Sousley
in his USMC dress blues.

Mike Strank,
in camouflage, on Bougainville.

Ira Hayes
in his USMC paratrooper gear.

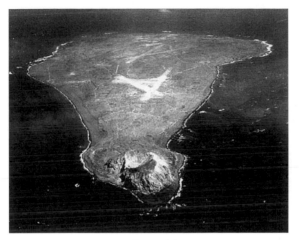

Iwo Jima, 1945.

D day, February 19, 1945—to the beaches,
with Mount Suribachi in the background.

The first flag is lowered as the second is raised.

The original Rosenthal photo, shot in a horizontal format, February 23, 1945. *Front row, left to right:* Ira Hayes, Franklin Sousley, Jack Bradley, Harlon Block. *Back row:* Mike Strank (behind Sousley) and Rene Gagnon (behind Bradley).

Papers across the country ran the photograph on February 25, 1945.

Felix de Weldon sculpting Rene Gagnon.

U.S. Marine Corps Memorial, Arlington, Virginia.

The Bradleys with commemorative plaque atop Mount Suribachi, April 1998.
From left to right: Betty, Steve, James, Joe, and Mark.

As he observed Sergeant Watson descending, Colonel Johnson calculated he could risk a larger force, and grabbed a field telephone. He called Dave Severance, who was bivouacked with Easy Company, still hugging the rocks on the southeastern point. "Send me a platoon!" Johnson ordered.

Severance surveyed his troops. The Second Platoon—Mike with Harlon, Franklin, and Ira—was off on a probe around Suribachi's base. The First was encamped several dozen yards away. So Severance chose the survivors of the Third (Doc's platoon), the closest to Colonel Johnson's command post, to become the first American platoon to climb the mountain. The ranks of the Third had been shredded by combat, so Severance augmented the group with twelve men from his machine-gun platoon and several men from the 60mm-mortar section. This increased the platoon strength to forty men.

Harry the Horse Liversedge himself picked the leader: First Lieutenant H. "George" Schrier, Severance's executive officer. Liversedge had known Schrier when they served in the Marine Raiders together. Just before the forty-man patrol began its climb, Colonel Johnson called Lieutenant Schrier aside and handed him an object from his map case. "If you get to the top," the colonel told Schrier, "put it up."

What Johnson handed the lieutenant was an American flag, one brought ashore from the USS *Missoula*. The flag was a relatively small one, measuring fifty-four by twenty-eight inches.

As the platoon got ready to climb, a Marine staff sergeant named Louis Lowery, a photographer for *Leatherneck* magazine, asked permission to come along and record the ascent on film. No one objected. The boys in the unit glanced upward, measuring what lay ahead.

"I thought I was sending them to their deaths," Dave Severance would later admit to me. "I thought the Japanese were waiting for a larger force."

As the forty-man line snaked upward, gained altitude, and grew visible against the near-vertical face of the mountain, Marines on the beaches and on the flat terrain to the north turned to watch. Even men aboard the offshore ships put binoculars to their eyes to follow the thin line's winding trek.

Nearly everyone had the same terrible thought: The Japanese were waiting for these boys and would cut them down.

The men on the march shared this sense of dread. Doc Bradley, shouldering his unit 3 bag, certainly worried about how many would return alive. "Down at the base, there wasn't one out of forty of us who expected to make it," he told an interviewer not long after the battle. "We all figured the Japanese would open up from caves all the way up to the crater."

And my father had an additional concern: "All the way up I kept wondering, how the devil was I going to get the casualties down?"

As the Marines climbed, they beheld Iwo Jima for the first time from the perspective of the Japanese. Spreading below them in panorama were the landing beaches and the armada at anchor in the ocean, the narrow neck they had secured at such cost, the enemy airstrip, and the rising terrain of the main bulk to the north. And the small figures that were their comrades, gazing back up at them.

About two-thirds of the way up, Lieutenant Schrier sent out flankers on either side of the main unit for cover. But it was completely quiet. Not a shot was fired. It took only forty minutes to get to the top.

The patrol clawed its way to the rim of the crater at about 10 A.M. Looking down into the bowl, the boys of the patrol saw devastation: Japanese antiaircraft guns fused together by the heat of American bombing, twisted metal, pulverized rock.

As everyone milled around at the top, Sergeant Hank Hansen relayed a request by Colonel Liversedge that Robert Leader, as the platoon's unofficial artist, make sketches of everything around him. Leader set to work. Then Boots Thomas came up with an order of his own: "See if you can find a pole to put the flag on."

Leader set aside his sketch pad, and he and another Marine named Leo Rozek scoured the rubble at their feet. The Japanese had constructed a catch system for rainwater on the crater's surface, and fragments of pipe lay scattered about. Rozek, rummaging in the mud, found a fragment of usable length. He and Leader lugged it upright. The two discovered a bullet hole in the pipe. The rope could be threaded through that.

Then, knowing that this was an important moment that would be photographed, the patrol's brass took over. Lieutenant Schrier, Sergeant Thomas, Sergeant Hansen, and Corporal Lindberg converged on the pole. They shook the folded flag out and tied it in place.

As Lou Lowery documented the proceedings with a steady succession of camera shots, another Marine, Louis Charlo, joined the four. At 10:20 A.M. the five men thrust the pole upright in the gusty wind, the first foreign flag ever to fly over Japanese soil.

Lowery, wanting added drama for his shot, motioned to Jim Michaels, who crouched dramatically in the foreground with his carbine. Then Lowery shouted, "Wait a minute!" He'd run out of film. As he reloaded, Lindberg scowled and grunted at him to hurry it up: Men holding flags were easy targets. With a fresh roll of film in his camera, Lowery called for a final, posed shot: Hansen, Thomas, and Schrier gripping the flagpole as they stiffly circled it, Lindberg and Charlo watching them from a couple of paces off, Michaels adding drama in the foreground with the gun.

As Lowery clicked this exposure, an amazing noise rose from the island below and from the ships offshore. Thousands of Marine and Navy personnel had been watching the patrol as they climbed to the volcano's rim. When the small swatch of color fluttered, Iwo Jima was transformed, for a few moments, into New York City's Times Square on New Year's Eve. Infantrymen cheered, whistled, and waved their helmets. Here was the evidence of Suribachi's conquest. Here was the first invader's flag ever planted in four thousand years on the soil of Japan.

In their giddiness, many of the young Marines watching from below assumed that the battle of Iwo Jima was now over. Robert Leader was one combatant who did not make this assumption. Amid the jubilation he experienced a chill of a darker sort. "When I saw the flag I thought it was a bad idea for us up there," he remembered. "It was like sitting in the middle of a bull's-eye."

Leader's misgivings quickly proved prophetic. Just moments after the Stars and Stripes went up, the summit of Hot Rocks got hot again. The first Japanese emerged from his tunnel with his back to the Marines. Harold Keller spotted him and fired his M1. The fallen figure was yanked back into the hole from where he'd come. Another sniper popped up, but he, too, was gunned down. Next was a maddened Japanese officer, who leaped into view with a broken sword; an alert Marine dropped him.

Photographer Lou Lowery was standing near the flag when a Japanese soldier stuck his head out of a cave and lobbed a grenade. Lowery dove over the volcano's rim and rolled and slid about forty feet down the steep, jagged side before he could break his fall. He suffered several cuts to his flesh but was not seriously injured. His camera was broken, but his film was safe. Lowery decided it was time to head back down to find another camera.

The firefight lasted several minutes, with no American casualties. And then the invisible enemy was silent again.

Only later would everyone comprehend just how much danger still festered inside Suribachi on that morning, February 23. Rummaging through an opened cave for souvenirs a few days afterward, Marines discovered the bodies of at least 150 Japanese, freshly dead. They had died of self-inflicted wounds. Many had killed themselves by holding grenades to their stomachs.

Why these Japanese hadn't tried to bolt from the cave and overwhelm the flag-raising patrol was a mystery. If they had followed the orders of General Kuribayashi, they would have fought to the death, killing as many Americans as possible. Perhaps the suicides could be explained as a corruption of the samurai ideal—the brainwashing of the *issen gorin* by a fanatical military establishment.

While the Third Platoon was taking control of Suribachi's summit, down below, the secretary of the Navy, James Forrestal, decided that he wanted to go ashore and witness the final stage of the fight for the mountain. Along with Howlin' Mad Smith, the secretary reached the beach just after the flag went up, and the mood among the high command turned jubilant.

Forrestal was so taken with the fervor of the moment that he decided he wanted the Suribachi flag as a souvenir. The news of this wish did not sit well with Chandler Johnson, whose temperament was every bit as fiery as Howlin' Mad's. Colonel Johnson felt that the flag belonged to the battalion of Marines who had sacrificed so many lives to make this conquest. He decided to secure the flag as soon as possible, and dispatched his assistant operations officer, Lieutenant Ted Tuttle, to the beach to scare up a replacement flag, possibly to give to Forrestal.

As an afterthought, Johnson called after Tuttle: "And make it a bigger one."

At about this same time, a short, nearsighted, mustachioed wire-service photographer named Joe Rosenthal was struggling through an uneven morning. Rosenthal, covering the invasion for the Associated Press, had slipped on a wet ladder and fallen into the ocean between the command ship and a landing craft. Fished out, he unzipped his camera—a bulky and durable Speed Graphic—from its waterproof bag and clicked off a shot of Forrestal and Smith looking resolutely toward the beach.

As Rosenthal was approaching Iwo Jima in a landing craft in the company of Bill Hipple, a magazine correspondent, the boatswain told Rosenthal he had just heard on his radio that a patrol was climbing Suribachi. Knowing a news story when they heard one, Hipple and Rosenthal headed toward the mountain. They moved slowly, careful to avoid marked mines, until they reached the command post of the Twenty-eighth Regiment. There they encountered two Marines who were also combat photographers: Private Bob Campbell, who worked with a still camera, and Sergeant Bill Genaust, who had a movie camera loaded with color film.

It was too late to capture the flag raising itself, but Rosenthal had come too far to turn back. "I'd still like to go up," he said to Sergeant Genaust, and talked Campbell and Genaust—who were armed—into making the ascent with him. The three men shouldered their cameras and hit the steep trail.

While Lieutenant Tuttle was off searching for a replacement flag, Chandler Johnson decided that Lieutenant Schrier, up on the mountain, could use a wired connection with the base for his field telephone, whose battery signal was growing weak. He rang up Dave Severance at Easy Company and ordered a detail to reel out a phone wire for Schrier.

The Second Platoon had just trooped in from its probe around the mountain's base. Severance ordered Mike, Harlon, Ira, and Franklin to the battalion command post to tie in a telephone wire that the team would then unreel up the mountain. The boys were tired, and uneasy about the Japanese, but nobody complained.

Severance also dispatched his runner, nineteen-year-old Rene Gagnon, to the command post for fresh SCR-300 batteries for Schrier.

Mike, Harlon, Ira, and Franklin reached Colonel Johnson's field headquarters just as Lieutenant Tuttle hurried into view. He was carrying an American flag that he had obtained from LST-779 on the beach. As it happened, this flag—which at ninety-six by fifty-six inches was a good deal larger than the one now planted on the mountain—had been found in a salvage yard at Pearl Harbor, rescued from a ship the Japanese had sunk on the infamous December morning.

Tuttle handed the flag to Chandler Johnson, who in turn gave it to Rene to put inside his field pack. "When you get to the top," the colonel told Mike Strank, who was standing near Rene, "you tell Schrier to put this flag up, and I want him to save the small flag for me."

With their cargo of batteries, the American flag, and telephone wire that they unreeled as they climbed, the five boys set off for the mountain summit, where my father had remained. The five reached the rim of the volcano around noon. Mike reported to Lieutenant Schrier, explained the delivery of wire and batteries, and told him of Johnson's desire to preserve the first flag.

As Rene handed Mike the replacement flag Mike decided an explanation was in order. "Colonel Johnson wants this big flag run up high," Mike told the lieutenant, "so that [everyone] on this whole cruddy island can see it!"

Mike directed Ira and Franklin to look for a second length of pipe. He and Harlon started clearing a spot for planting the pole, and Harlon began stacking stones. On his descent from the crater, Lowery encountered Joe Rosenthal, Bill Genaust, and Bob Campbell, the three photographers, picking their way upward. Lowery told the group that he'd already photographed the flag raising.

The three photographers considered turning around and heading back. But Lowery had a different idea. "You should go on up there," he said, adding that the view from the top was spectacular. The three nodded and trudged on.

A good view of a different sort greeted Rosenthal when he reached the summit: the American flag, in close-up, snapping in the strong breeze. "I tell you, I still get this feeling of a patriotic jolt when I recall seeing our flag flying up there," he told an interviewer some years later.

Then Rosenthal spotted another interesting sight toward the far side of the crater: a couple of Marines hauling an iron pole toward another Marine, who was holding a second American flag, neatly folded.

Rosenthal's fingers instinctively went to his Speed Graphic. Maybe he would get a flag-raising photograph after all. Not the original, not the first, but a flag raising nonetheless.

The pole that Ira and Franklin were dragging was a length of drainage pipe that weighed more than a hundred pounds. As they approached the site, Lieutenant Schrier suggested that Mike's team do the job. The lieutenant wanted the replacement flag raised simultaneously with the lowering of the first one.

Mike attached the flag to the pole. Schrier rounded up some Marines to lower the first pole, and then stood between the two clusters of flag groups, directing them.

The three photographers milled about some distance away, near the volcano's rim. Each of the three looked for a good vantage point. The five-foot-five Rosenthal had put down his Speed Graphic and was bent over, piling up stones and a sandbag to stand on and improve his shooting angle.

His camera was set at a speed of 1/400th of a second, with the f-stop between 8 and 16.

No one else on the summit paid much attention to what was going on. It all happened in seconds and was recorded by Genaust's movie camera. In the solitude of my living room I have watched those few seconds again and again, in slow motion. Here is how the event unfolded:

Harlon braced himself above the target spot in the rubble-strewn ground, ready to receive the base of the pole. Mike, at the other end, in charge, guided it toward him, the pipe over his right shoulder.

Mike held the large flag wrapped around the pole to keep it from fluttering in the strong wind until the pole was planted.

Mike and his four squad members circled closer to the pole. They raised their feet high with each step, to get clear of the debris. It looked as if they were walking in deep snow. Ira walked toward the pole, facing Mike, his back to Genaust's camera frame. He said something to Mike that was lost in the strong wind. In typical fashion for Ira, he was wearing his Indian-style blanket, stuffed through his military belt on his rump.

Mike saw Doc Bradley walking past with a load of bandages in his arms and asked him to come and help. Doc dropped the bandages and moved to the pole, directly between Mike and Harlon.

Franklin walked to the pole from the foreground of Genaust's camera frame.

Rene approached the group from behind, to the right, his rifle slung over his shoulder. He stood behind my father, who was in front of the pole in the movie frame. The boys converged in a cluster behind Harlon, who bent low at the base. Doc gripped the pole in the cluster's center.

Rosenthal spotted the movement and swung his camera up and clicked off a frame. In that same instant the flagpole rose upward in a quick arc. The banner, released from Mike's grip, fluttered out in the strong wind.

And then it was over. The flag was up.

Campbell had gotten the shot he was after: the first flag going down, in the foreground of his frame, and the second one going up, off in the distance. Genaust had gotten the footage he wanted: a routine, spontaneous color sequence of the replacement flag being raised.

Only Joe Rosenthal was unsure. He had clicked the camera just once. The AP man hadn't even had a chance to glimpse the image in his viewfinder. He'd captured 1/400th of a second out of four seconds of fluid motion. Just one exposure. He had no idea whether he'd gotten a blur, a shot of the sky, or a passable photograph.

The six continued to struggle with the heavy pole in the whipping wind. The pole was fully upright. Harlon raised his hands up on the pole and gripped it as he would a baseball bat, using his weight to force it into the ground. Ira did the same. Then Franklin added his heft. Mike anchored things.

Within a few more seconds the flagpole was freestanding, the cloth snapping and cracking in the wind. After a moment Franklin and some of the others began looking for rocks to add support. Doc offered ropes he'd brought along to tie casualties to stretchers, and they secured the pole.

No one paid attention. It was just a replacement flag. The important flag—the first one raised that day—was brought down the mountain and presented to Colonel Johnson, who stored it in the battalion safe. It bore too much historic value for it to be left unguarded atop Suribachi.

The replacement flag flew for three weeks, eventually chewed up by the strong winds.

A few moments after the raising, Joe Rosenthal did what Lowery had done a couple of hours before him. He called several Marines over to cluster around the pole for a standard "gung-ho" shot. Lieutenant Schrier helped gather a crowd of boys for this photograph. Mike, Ira, Doc, Franklin, and fourteen other Marines posed proudly beneath the flag, waving their arms, rifles, and helmets.

Doc Bradley would later say, "We were happy," and in this shot he looks it. He has a big smile as he waves his helmet with his right hand.

Joe Rosenthal was satisfied with this staged shot. He felt certain that with all these smiling young boys facing the camera and the landing beaches visible below, he had a photograph that would make the papers back home.

TWELVE

Myths

Here's one for all time!

—John Bodkin, AP photo editor in Guam

Joe Rosenthal's pack of film from February 23, with twelve exposures, together with a pack he had started shooting the day before, began to work its way through the military channels back to America. First it was tossed into a mail plane headed for the base at Guam, a thousand miles south across the Pacific. There the film would pass through many hands, any of which could consign it to a wastebasket. Technicians from a press pool lab would develop it. Their mistakes were routinely tossed aside. Then censors would scrutinize it, and finally the pool chief would look at each print to decide which was worth transmitting back to the States.

Of the twelve exposures from the pack taken on the twenty-third, two were ruined by streaks from light that had leaked through the camera housing onto the film. These two

115

were adjacent to the tenth frame, the one Rosenthal had clicked off without looking into the viewfinder. For some reason the light hadn't marred that one.

Three days after the flag raising, resting with the other members of Easy Company after one of history's most ferocious battles, my father found time to write home.

Iwo Jima
Feb 26, 1945

Dear Mother, Dad & all,

    I just have time for a line or two, I want to tell you I am in the best of health. You know all about our battle out here and I was with the victorious Co. E. 2nd Batt 28th Marines who reached the top of Mt. Suribachi first. I had a little to do with raising the American flag and it was the happiest moment of my life. . . .
    I'd give my left arm for a good shower and a clean shave, I have a 6 day beard. Haven't had any soap or water since I hit the beach. I never knew I could go without food, water, or sleep for three days but I know now, it can be done.
    I'll write a longer letter when I get the chance, good luck and give everyone my regards.

Your loving son,
Jack

Franklin wrote to Goldie, offering her a harrowing kind of reassurance: that she shouldn't worry, even though bullets had been whizzing through his clothes.

Iwo Jima
February 27, 1945

Dearest Mother,

As you probably already know we hit Iwo Jima February 19th just a week ago today. My regiment took the hill with our company on the front line. The hill was hard and I sure never expected war to be like it was those first 4 days. . . . There is some heavy fighting on one end and we are bothered some at night. . . . Look for my picture because I helped put the flag up. Please don't worry and write.

> Your son,
> Franklin Sousley
> US Marine

Like Rosenthal, Franklin hoped the posed "gung-ho" shot in which he appeared would make the papers back home. He had already told those he was close to that he wanted to come home a hero.

Rene took a moment to jot a note to his sweetheart, Pauline Harnois:

Now that I can tell you, I was in action on Iwo Jima and that is the reason for such a delay in writing. I am still fine and some of my buddies are still with me, some are dead or wounded. . . . I got your pictures with the evening gown aboard ship so I put them in my helmet and carried them with me. They're not banged up too much. You still look beautiful, darling.

The Marines on Suribachi could not know it, but back home Iwo Jima had become the number-one front-page story, not to mention the most heavily covered battle in World War II.

In all invasions before this, news copy had "hitchhiked" back to America on whatever transportation was available. Usually it had been flown to Honolulu on hospital planes evacuating the wounded. Often days went by before news hit the home front.

But at Iwo Jima the process was accelerated. Covering the invasion were far more journalists—fresh from the European theater, which was winding down—than had watched Bougainville or Tarawa. And they sent their dispatches quickly. Daily editions during the week of February 19 brought battle accounts within twenty-four hours of actual time. Suddenly civilians clustered in coffee shops and gathered around watercoolers were bantering with ease about Green Beach, Suribachi, and Kuribayashi.

On the day after the invasion, February 20, and for the rest of the week, Iwo Jima remained the top news story. Tuesday's main headline in *The New York Times* blared, "Marines Fight Way to Airfield on Iwo Isle; Win 2-Mile Beachhead; 800 Ships Aid Landing."

It hardly seemed to matter that General Patton was racing across Germany or that President Roosevelt was sailing back from a historic summit in the Crimea. All other news was secondary to that from Iwo Jima. Wednesday's *Times* headline offered a hint of triumph: "Marines Conquer Airfield, Hold Third of Iwo."

The joyous mood was tempered by General Smith's somber front-page quote that made plain the scale of the bloodletting: "The fight is the toughest we've run across in 168 years."

On Thursday the banner headline brought more sobering news: Marines halted on Iwo, near first airfield. And on page four of *The New York Times*, in an article headlined "Marines' Hardest Fight," the grisly statistics began to unspool:

> Now the Marines have come to their hardest battle, a battle still un-won. Our first waves on Iwo were almost wiped out; 3,650 Marines were dead, wounded or missing after only two days of fighting on the most heavily defended island in the world, more than the total casualties of Tarawa, about as many as all the Marine casualties of Guadalcanal in the five months of jungle combat

While Friday and Saturday newspaper headlines remained disheartening, the image of Joe Rosenthal's flag raisers was under the scrutiny of John Bodkin, the AP photo editor in Guam. On a routine night in his bureau office he casually picked up a glossy print of the photograph. He looked at it. He paused, shook his head in wonder, and whistled. "Here's one for all time!" he exclaimed to those around him.

Without wasting a second, Bodkin radioed the image to AP headquarters in New York. Soon wirephoto machines in newsrooms across the country were picking up the AP image. Newspaper editors, accustomed to sorting through endless battle photographs, would cast an idle glance at it, then take a second look. "Lead photo, page one, above the fold," they would bark.

News pros were not the only ones bedazzled by the photo. Captain T. B. Clark of the Navy was on duty at Patuxent Air Station in Virginia that Saturday when it came humming off the wire. He studied it for a minute, then thrust it under the gaze of Petty Officer Felix de Weldon, an Austrian immigrant who was a painter and sculptor. De Weldon was assigned to Patuxent's studios to paint a mural of the battle of the Coral Sea.

The young artist could not take his eyes off the flag-raising photo. In its classic triangular lines he recognized similarities with the great ancient statues he had studied. He reflexively reached for some sculptor's clay and tools. With the photograph before him, he labored through the long night. By dawn he had replicated the six boys pushing a pole, raising a flag.

The next morning, Sunday, February 25, millions of Americans were similarly transfixed by the image. People would always remember where they were the moment they saw the photo. It signaled victory and hope, a counterpoint to the photos of sinking ships at Pearl Harbor that had signaled defeat and fear four years earlier.

Harlon's brother Ed Block Jr., home on leave from the Air Force, had just sat down and lifted the Sunday paper in front of him when Belle breezed into the room. As she passed behind him she glanced at the paper. Then she stopped. She leaned over Ed's right shoulder, put her finger on the figure in the photo thrusting the pole into the ground, and exclaimed: "Looky there, Junior! There's your brother Harlon!"

Ed did a double take, looking hard at the photo. The figure Belle was pointing to was unidentifiable, just the back of a Marine with no side view. The caption read only "Old Glory Goes up over Iwo," and the articles provided no names.

"Momma," Ed declared, "there's no way you can know that's Harlon. That's just the back of a Marine. And besides, we don't even know Harlon is on Iwo Jima."

"Oh, that's definitely Harlon," Belle insisted as she slid the paper from Ed's grasp. And as she strode into the kitchen, her eyes fixed on the photo, Ed could hear her saying, "I know my boy."

The photograph's impact spread like a shock wave.

No one knew who the flag raisers were, but Joe Rosenthal was an instant celebrity. On February 27 the *Times* ran a huge photo of Joe, identifying him as the photographer "who has earned nationwide praise for his picture." By national consensus, it was a beautiful image. But for those who wanted facts, what, exactly, did it represent? No one suspected it, but the photograph suggested a very different reality from that being experienced by the Marines back on Iwo Jima.

And a number of elements, a lot of them tinged with irony, came together to create a set of myths for the American public.

First, thousands of Marines and sailors had cheered the initial flag raising atop Suribachi, but from a distance. Only a few were close enough to see exactly who the raisers were. No one paid attention to or cheered the raising of the replacement flag. And no one cared who raised it. For most of the Marines on the island, there was only one flag raising.

Second, because Rosenthal's AP photos traveled faster than Lowery's military photos, only one flag raising was represented in the papers back home.

Third, because the raising of the replacement flag was essentially a nonevent, little was said about it. So readers back home assumed there was only one flag raising—not the one the

Marines and sailors witnessed, but the one on the front pages of their newspapers.

Fourth, reporters safe on ships miles from Suribachi and editors half a world away not only failed to report the full range of facts, but unintentionally created a confusing portrait of the flag raisings.

These reporters had lavished great detail on the fierce fighting that led the Marines to the base of the mountain. Then they added three days of fanciful and garbled accounts of a murderous fight up Suribachi's slopes. But they never mentioned the actual, quiet walk up Suribachi on Friday morning, February 23. On that day, lacking any supporting photos of the conquest, the editors substituted a photograph of Marines pinned down on a hill far to the north. This only added to the myth that Marines had been exposed to fire on Suribachi's slopes. The public came to believe that not only was Suribachi conquered after the fiercest of fighting, but once conquered, the fighting on the entire island was virtually over.

When Rosenthal's photograph sprang into the nation's consciousness on that Sunday morning, it fused with the accumulated myth and seemed to depict a final triumph in the very teeth of battle.

How to explain this travesty of accuracy? How could an unopposed forty-minute climb up a hill and a quiet flag raising be portrayed as a valiant fight to the death? No Marines were quoted as sources, and none have since been blamed for the misleading hyperbole. Simply put, the press substituted romanticism for good reporting. Inflated stories of heroism made for better copy than the plain facts.

The flag raising did not signify the end of the battle. Easy Company's sector was secure, but no place was safe on the small island. The fighting would continue for a full month before Iwo Jima would be considered totally under American control.

On Wednesday, February 28, the Twenty-eighth Marines received orders to prepare to move north. On that evening Tex Stanton dropped into a foxhole that he and Mike Strank had prepared earlier. Mike was already there, and Stanton at once sensed something different about him.

"He was lying limp, hobo style, on his back with his hands behind his head," Stanton remembered. "And he was quiet. Now, Mike was always active, always talking, and I had never seen him still. So I asked, 'What's the matter?' Mike answered, 'Oh, nothing. I was just wondering where we're going with all this.' "

Tex Stanton felt a chill. He was so affected that he jumped out of the foxhole. "He was talking about his death," Tex maintained years later.

The northern battlefield beckoned to the remaining boys of Easy Company. The idyll atop Suribachi was about to end.

THIRTEEN

"We Gave Our Today"

They are saying, "The generals learned their lesson in the last war. There are going to be no wholesale slaughters." I ask, how is victory possible except by wholesale slaughters?

—Evelyn Waugh, in his 1939 diary

With the Stars and Stripes flying triumphantly over Suribachi, the American public may have thought the island was conquered, but the worst was far from over. On March 1, Easy Company, rested after the conquest of Suribachi, was ready to join the great offensive on the northern plateau. It plunged into action with the rest of the Twenty-eighth Marines along the embattled west coast, in the Fifth Division's zone of operations. It was nasty business. The terrain—rocky plateaus abutting steep cliffs and ravines—offered the usual absence of cover. The Twenty-eighth threw all three of its battalions onto the line, and the hidden Japanese gunners resumed their harvest.

Mike Strank was leading Ira, Harlon, Franklin, and other Marines across a dangerous strip of ground when a cluster of Japanese snipers opened up on them. Mike and some others dove behind an outcropping that seemed to give them solid protection from three sides. Its only exposure was toward the sea, where the U.S. fleet lay anchored.

As the heavy sniper fire continued, Mike sized up the situation. Pee Wee Griffiths, L. B. Holly, and Franklin bent toward their leader, awaiting orders. Mike talked to them about possible escape routes. Then he seemed to drift into a private place. He broke his own silence after a moment with a cryptic remark to L. B.: "You know, Holly, that's going to be one hell of an experience." L. B. waited for him to continue, then finally asked: "What are you talking about?" Mike did not reply; he only pointed to a dead Marine who sprawled a few feet from the group.

"He was telling me he would die," Holly reflected many years later. "And sure enough, two minutes later Mike was dead."

Joe Rodriguez watched it happen at close range; he was nearly killed himself. "Mike hollered at me to come over," he recalled. "He was on one knee with Franklin and the other guys around, getting ready to draw a plan in the sand to get us out of there. But before he could get a word out, a shell exploded."

Franklin and Holly were bowled over by the blast but were uninjured. Pee Wee was hit in the face and shoulder and temporarily blinded. Rodriguez woke up a few seconds later with "a warm feeling in my chest, unable to move my legs."

Mike Strank did not wake up. No Japanese could claim credit for this kill. In another irony of the battle for Iwo Jima, the shell that killed Mike had almost certainly come from a U.S. destroyer; it sliced through the only unprotected side of the outcropping. The Czech immigrant to America, born on the Marine Corps birthday, serving his third tour of duty for his adopted country, was cut down by friendly fire.

Progress was slow and lethal across the rocky, windswept plain. The Twenty-eighth was pinned down for four hours, its boys getting picked off with sickening regularity, before it could start moving again. And movement without cover offered only more danger. Easy Company, strung out in a long line, scampered across the hard rock toward the island's northern tip. The gunfire directed at them was intermittent but deadly. My father was following Hank Hansen across a crust of exposed ground when he saw Hank crumple. At first Doc thought the sergeant had tripped and fallen. But Hansen did not get up, so Doc ran to him and pulled him into a nearby shell crater.

The bullet had entered Hansen's back and exited through his abdomen. "It was a bad wound," my father told a magazine interviewer a few months later, "but one thing you learn out there is not to give up. I yelled for somebody to hold the plasma bottle while I put a battle dressing on. For me, it was the luckiest thing I ever did."

Hansen was dying, but Doc's cry for assistance saved his own life. Tex Hipps came sliding into the crater to assist the corpsman. Then he glanced over Doc's shoulder and shouted, "Watch out, Bradley!" Four Japanese, one brandishing a sword, were charging him, screaming, *"Banzai!"* Hipps dropped the sword-wielding officer and one soldier with his MI; the other two retreated.

Having escaped another brush with death, my father turned his attention back to Hank. As his friend lay near death, John Bradley removed Hank's wristwatch and promised to get it to his loved ones back home.

Harlon Block's role as heir to Mike Strank lasted until dusk. As twilight settled in, the rawboned Texan moved among the boys of what was now his squad, giving orders for everyone to dig in. Tex Stanton had secured himself in his foxhole when Harlon—his helmet characteristically tilted to one side— walked up to the rim and asked about one of his men, "Where's Hauskins?"

"Over there," Stanton replied, and then added, "You'd better get down, Harlon."

"Then Harlon just exploded," Melvin Duncan remembered. "He was blown into the air; there was dust and debris all around him."

The All–South Texas pass catcher, the boy who'd ridden along the banks of the Rio Grande on his white horse, stood there a moment, his hands filled with a heavy redness. His back—which formed one of the most galvanic contours in the flag-raising photograph—now lay limp. A few days earlier he had written a letter to Belle saying that he had come through the battle without a scratch, but it had not yet left the island. Its postal cancellation would eventually read March 14.

On the day Mike and Harlon died, Congressman Joseph Hendricks of Florida, holding up the now-famous photograph of the flag raisers, introduced a bill authorizing the erection of a monument "to the heroic action of the Marine Corps as typified by the Marines in this photograph. I have provided in the bill that this picture be a model for the monument."

At the same time Maurine Block was imploring her mother,

Belle, not to keep telling everyone that it was Harlon in the photograph at the base of the flagpole. It was just the back of a Marine. No one could be sure which one.

But Belle was sure. Her reply to Maurine was a mother's: "I changed so many diapers on that boy's butt. I know it's my boy."

The mission of Easy Company on March 2 and 3 was to advance on a series of low, stony ridges cut through with shallow ravines, filled with piles of rubble. Japanese shooters populated these ridges, using natural cover as well as their maze of caves and tunnels.

By March 3 some sixteen thousand of the original twenty-two thousand Japanese defenders were still alive. The Americans had taken sixteen thousand casualties, with three thousand dead. The Second Battalion's feisty colonel, Chandler Johnson—who had saved the original flag on Suribachi for his men—became one of four of the Twenty-eighth's seven officers killed that day. It was one of the bloodiest days of the campaign.

Nobody was safe. Sergeant Boots Thomas, who had led the thrust to the mountain's base and was interviewed on CBS radio, took a field telephone handed to him by Phil Ward. As he answered the call, a sniper shot his rifle out of his right hand. Thomas did not flinch. The next shot ripped through his mouth, killing him instantly.

The fighting was cramped and vicious. Five men of the Fifth Division were awarded the Medal of Honor on this day, a record unmatched in modern warfare. In addition to those awarded medals, there were countless acts of heroism, some officially documented, some barely noticed, that defined the essence of what it was to be a Marine.

It was on March 4 that the lacerated, exhausted Americans saw the first demonstration of why they were fighting and dying on the ugly little island. A crippled B-29 returning from an attack on Tokyo became the first American plane to make an emergency landing on Iwo Jima. Nearby Marines watched with astonishment as the crew leaped from the aircraft and kissed the ground. The ground was shaking with artillery fire. As far as the leathernecks were concerned, the crew had just landed in an inferno. They got a different perspective when one of the crewmen, thankful he had been spared a crash landing in the Pacific, shouted: "Thank God for you Marines!"

Joe Rosenthal landed on Guam on that day and unintentionally created another myth about the flag raising: the myth that his world-famous photograph was staged. As he later recounted: "When I walked into press headquarters, a correspondent walked up to me. 'Congratulations, Joe,' he said, 'on that flag-raising shot on Iwo.'

" 'Thanks,' I said.

" 'It's a great picture,' he said. 'Did you pose it?'

" 'Sure,' I said.

"I thought he meant the group shot I had arranged with the Marines waving and cheering, but then someone else came up with the flag-raising picture and I saw it for the first time.

" 'Gee,' I said. 'That's good, all right, but I didn't pose it. I wish I could take credit for posing it, but I can't.'

"Had I posed the shot, I would, of course, have ruined it. I would have picked fewer men, for the six are so crowded in the picture that one of them—Sergeant Michael Strank—only the hands are visible."

This conversation would haunt Rosenthal for the rest of his life. Some of the correspondents listening to him assumed that he was talking not about the "gung-ho" photograph, but about the previous frame, the one that was now so famous. Soon a false and damaging slur was making the rounds: that the photo of the raising of the replacement flag, universally understood as the only flag-raising photograph, was staged. (Lou Lowery's shot of the original raising, delayed in its transmission to the United States, never made an impact on the public consciousness.)

As soon as he arrived back in the States, Joe Rosenthal did his best to set the record straight. In the next fifty years, no matter how many times he tried to explain, Joe Rosenthal's 1/400th-second exposure would bring him nearly as much frustration as it did satisfaction.

Back on the island, the Marines were taking terrible casualties, but at least one Japanese saw clearly how it would all end. General Kuribayashi sent a radio message to Tokyo: Iwo Jima would soon fall, resulting in "scenes of disaster in our empire. However, I comfort myself in seeing my officers and men die without regret after struggling in this inch-by-inch battle."

My father's luck continued to hold. Sometime on March 4 he narrowly escaped death once again. He was treating a wounded

Marine in a shell hole, my father told my brother Tom, when he glanced up to see a Japanese soldier charging him with a bayonet.

"I shot him with my pistol," John Bradley recalled later.

But some of those closest to Doc were not so lucky. After this incident Doc returned to his platoon, but he could not find his special pal Iggy. Ralph Ignatowski had been walking with Doc just before he went to help the Marine in the shell hole. Now he was gone. Doc asked a few Marines in the area about Iggy's whereabouts. No one knew.

The next day, with fresh Marines joining the fray, Captain Severance took Easy Company back south, toward Suribachi. He was taking his boys for a brief, well-deserved rest. On the western beaches, across the island from the landing side, Dave's battle-scarred kids stacked their rifles and plunged into the surf for a bit of swimming.

During Easy Company's respite, my father continued to wonder about Iggy. He asked around; none of the other boys had seen him. The mystery gnawed at him. Teamwork was encoded into the Marines' behavior. Iggy would not have simply left the company without saying something to someone.

On March 7, Easy moved out again, headed for the northern killing fields. On the same day, back in the United States, Representative Mike Mansfield of Montana, a future ambassador to Japan, made a proposal to Congress that fired the imagination of his colleagues. Another in the series of national bond tours—elaborate coast-to-coast touring shows, organized by the Treasury Department—was being put together to raise money for the war effort. The governmental sale of war bonds to the public had financed America's involvement in both world wars.

Mansfield called for the flag-raising image to be adopted as a symbol of this tour, so that "we as a people would do our part in keeping the flag flying at home as they have done in keeping it flying on foreign battlefields." His motion was carried with great enthusiasm.

On March 8 the Marines of Easy Company found Iggy. He had been grabbed, probably from behind, and pulled into a cave of Japanese soldiers. As the company medic, it was my father's job to deal with what remained of Iggy's body after three days of brutal torture. He had to have been sickened when he imagined what Iggy endured. I feel certain that the shock my young father must have experienced added greatly to his near-total silence, for the rest of his life, regarding his memories of the war.

The Twenty-eighth spent the next day clawing its way northward for about 150 yards, alternating intervals of monotony and danger. The day after was a virtual repetition. The incessant fighting against a concealed enemy, harsh weather, heavy casualties, and general fatigue were beginning to take their toll on the Marines. The boys had begun to resemble ghostly remnants of a fighting force. Scruffy beards matted their faces. Their fatigues were ripped and stiff with accumulated sweat. One man would later write that their lips were puffed and black and their mouths hung open, as if they were having trouble breathing.

But as the boys slogged through their seemingly endless operation on Iwo Jima, the effects of what they had accomplished began to change the contours of the Pacific War. On March 9 more than three hundred B-29s, now free of harassment from the Japanese planes that had been flying out of Iwo Jima's airstrips, launched the first of the great firebombing raids on Tokyo. The casualty figures from this and other firebombing raids would be higher than those caused by the nuclear attacks on Hiroshima and Nagasaki five months later.

The Marines inched forward on Iwo Jima's hard shell. My father continued to rush to the aid of casualties under heavy fire. On March 11 two companies covered twenty-five yards and took thirty-three casualties; on the twelfth they were stalled, with twenty-seven casualties. It was that kind of fighting.

And on this day Doc Bradley's war came to an end. Sam Trussell, who was wounded along with Doc, remembered it. The two were crouching at the base of a cliff with other Marines. They thought they were protected by an overhang, but the mortar shell that got them smashed against a flat rock and sent steel splinters flying.

"I was blinded," Trussell recalled, "and Doc pulled me back into the hole. Then he worked on a guy whose legs were torn up. Then he guided me to the aid station. I heard some guys talking about Doc's bloody legs, but I couldn't see how bad he was hit."

My father had taken shrapnel wounds to his right thigh, calf, and foot, and to his left foot. This did not stop him at first. Rolla Perry recalled glimpsing him as he ran past the enclosure: Both his legs were bleeding, but he was busily treating five other wounded Marines. Doc was eventually taken to the battalion aid station for emergency treatment, then on to the field hospital, where some of the fragments were removed. The next morning he was loaded onto a plane for Guam and then sent to a hospital in Hawaii.

In the Pacific killing grounds Doc Bradley was just one of

thousands of casualties. But back in the United States, millions of people were scrutinizing his profile in Rosenthal's photograph, wondering who he and the other flag raisers were. The New York *Sun* had superimposed a drawing of the famous "Spirit of '76" illustration in one corner of the photo. After it hit the newsstands, forty-eight thousand people sent in requests for copies.

The day after my father departed, Rene Gagnon fired his rifle for the first time. He and a buddy had wandered into a cave, assuming it was empty. The two boys found themselves facing a lone Japanese soldier with his rifle aimed at them. As he told his son, Rene junior, he had a blinding thought in the split second that followed: "We all have mothers. We're all human. Why does this have to be?"

The enemy soldier fired first. Rene's buddy dropped dead. In the next second it would be Rene's turn. He squeezed the trigger, and the Japanese crumbled. Rene stood in the cave, trembling. This was what the battle had come down to. To his son, he later recalled thinking: "Why did I have to do this? Looking down a barrel into someone's eyeballs and having to kill him. There's no glory in it."

On March 14 Admiral Chester W. Nimitz proclaimed Iwo Jima conquered and that "all powers of government of the Japanese Empire in these islands are hereby suspended." Two days later Nimitz declared Iwo officially secured and said that organized Japanese resistance had ended.

"Who does the admiral think he's kidding?" steamed Marine

private Bob Campbell when he heard of this. "We're still getting killed!" James Buchanan recalled of those closing days. "We were trapped!" he said of his unit. "Getting shot at constantly. I was a private, and replacements were reporting to me. There was no one else left."

On March 16 General Kuribayashi radioed Tokyo: "The battle is approaching its end. Since the enemy's landing, even the gods would weep at the bravery of the officers and men under my command."

On that same day Louis Ruppel, the executive editor of the Chicago *Herald American*, had a brainstorm and sent a telegram to his friend in the White House, Franklin Delano Roosevelt: Why not use the flag raisers captured in Joe Rosenthal's photograph as stars of the bond tour?

The photograph had created such a stir that the president of the United States was about to anoint the flag raisers government-approved national heroes. Yet no one knew who they were or what they had done.

Amid all his command duties, Captain Dave Severance of Easy Company received a strange request from Washington that distracted if not annoyed him: Could he please provide the names of the Marines in Rosenthal's photograph? "We were fighting for survival," Severance told me. "Naming the flag raisers was a subject far from my mind."

By this time newspaper clippings of the flag-raising photograph had made their way to the island. Keyes Beech, a Marine correspondent, was one of many journalists who saw a story in finding the flag raisers. But the Easy boys who had been atop Suribachi that day were by now either casualties or scattered in the northern fighting. Only the runner, Rene Gagnon, was available to help Beech with the identification.

Rene scrutinized the figures for the correspondent. His best guess was five names: Franklin Sousley, Mike Strank, John Bradley, himself, and Henry Hansen. Rene had determined that Hansen was the figure on the far right, ramming the pole into the ground with his back to the camera. Ira Hayes and Harlon Block were not mentioned.

By March 21 the invasion force on Iwo Jima had been attacking for thirty-one consecutive days—a sustained effort unique in modern warfare. Their daily mission was unchanged: move on to one more ridge. The battle was for yards, feet, and sometimes even inches—brutal, deadly, and dangerous combat aimed at an underground, heavily fortified, nonretreating enemy. Five days of fighting remained, but no one could know that. Sleep-deprived, undernourished, hardened to the routine of constant death, the boys shuffled forward in a trancelike state.

Perhaps that explains what happened to Franklin Sousley.

Franklin had grown in battle, his comrades had observed. He'd seemed to get older and bigger. The last time L. B. Holly saw him, the young boy from Kentucky was cradling a wounded Marine between his legs as a corpsman gave first aid. A hell of a good Marine, Holly thought. A very considerate boy.

Then Franklin lost his focus, for just a moment. The island had nearly been secured. Some Marines were already reboarding the transport ships offshore. And Franklin simply wandered onto a road. It was a known area of Japanese sniper fire. Perhaps Franklin forgot that. Perhaps he figured the Japanese had stopped shooting. Perhaps he was daydreaming about his girl.

The shot got him from behind. As the boys around him dove

to the ground, Franklin swatted absently at his back, as though brushing away a blue-tailed fly. Then he fell.

Someone shouted to him: "How ya doin'?" and Franklin answered back, "Not bad. I don't feel anything." And then he died.

The glassy-eyed Marines had been inflicting heavy enemy losses for many days; as usual, these losses were mostly concealed from the Marines' view. But now the signs were inescapable that final victory was near.

"We are still fighting," Kuribayashi radioed on March 22. "The strength under my command is now about four hundred. Tanks are attacking us. The enemy suggested we surrender through a loudspeaker, but our officers and men just laughed and paid no attention."

It was Kuribayashi's last dispatch. His body was never found. His abandoned blockhouse was blown up on the day Franklin died. The job required four tons of explosives.

The Japanese defenders grew reckless in their desperation. Enemy infiltrators were everywhere at night now, providing easy targets for Marine sharpshooters. A banzai charge on the night of March 22 faltered, with fifty of the sixty attackers gunned down. Area after area on the northern plateau was declared "secure"—each area having been won at appalling cost.

Three days after that, the war was over for Easy Company. Easy's original total force on Iwo Jima was 310 young men, including replacements. On March 26 Captain Severance led his 50 survivors on a tour of the newly dedicated Fifth Division cemetery. After wiping away their tears, they traveled by small boat to the transport, the *Winged Arrow*, for the trip back home. They had to climb a cargo net to get aboard. Many were so weak that they had to be pulled over the rail by sailors.

Severance was the only one of six Easy Company officers to walk off the island. Easy Company had suffered 84 percent casualties.

Of the eighteen triumphant boys in Joe Rosenthal's "gung-ho" flag-raising photograph, fourteen were casualties.

The hard statistics show the sacrifice made by Colonel Johnson's Second Battalion: 1,400 boys landed on D day and 288 replacements were provided as the battle went on, for a total of 1,688. Of these, 1,511 had been killed or wounded. Only 177 walked off the island. And of the final 177, 91 had been wounded at least once and returned to battle.

It had taken twenty-two crowded transports to bring the Fifth Division to the island. The survivors fit comfortably onto eight departing ships.

The American boys had killed about twenty-one thousand Japanese but suffered more than twenty-six thousand casualties in the process. This would be the only battle in the Pacific where the invaders suffered higher casualties than the defenders.

The Marines fought in World War II for forty-three months. Yet in one month on Iwo Jima, one-third of their total deaths occurred. Thousands of families would not have the solace of a body to bid farewell to, only the abstract information that the Marine had "died in the performance of his duty" and was buried in a plot, aligned in a row with numbers on his grave. Mike lay in Plot 3, Row 5, Grave 694; Harlon in Plot 4, Row 6, Grave 912; Franklin in Plot 8, Row 7, Grave 2,189.

When I think of Mike, Harlon, and Franklin there, I think of the message someone had chiseled outside the cemetery:

When you go home
Tell them for us and say
For your tomorrow
We gave our today

Most of the Japanese dead lay sealed in caves, where they would be mummified by sulfur fumes. Decades later, many would be found perfectly preserved, their eyeglasses still on. In the 1,364 days from Pearl Harbor to the Japanese surrender, with millions of Americans fighting on global battlefronts, 353 Americans were awarded Medals of Honor, the nation's highest decoration for valor. Marines accounted for eighty-four of these decorations, with an astonishing twenty-seven awarded for just one month's action on Iwo Jima, a record unsurpassed by any battle in U.S. history. Iwo Jima stands as America's most heroic battle.

FOURTEEN

Antigo

I knew nothing of all this, growing up in Antigo. I knew almost nothing of it until after my father's death in 1994.

World War II had been over less than ten years when I was born. Yet from a boy's perspective in this small, tree-shaded town, it might as well have been fought in the Middle Ages— vivid and glorious, but already distant, a kind of myth.

This sense of distance was a little strange, of course, given that we all knew, early on, that our father was a figure in the most famous war photograph ever made. But that's all we knew. Our father himself never mentioned the photograph. No copies of it existed in the house. The names Mike, Harlon, Ira, Franklin, and Rene were unknown to us, as was the name Iggy.

· · ·

My father had come home from the war and looked up his childhood sweetheart, Elizabeth Van Gorp, of Appleton, Wisconsin. They married in May of 1946 and moved to Milwaukee, where he worked at a funeral home while studying mortuary science. They set up house in a chauffeur's quarters above a four-car garage. In 1947 their first child, Kathy, was born, and John heard of an opening at the Muttart McGillan Funeral Home in Antigo. He brought Betty and the baby to his hometown. He probably carried in his pocket all the money he possessed.

Seven years later, at the age of thirty-two, he was able to make one of the biggest commercial purchases in the county's history: the McCandless & Zobel Funeral Home. He made the front page of the Antigo *Daily Journal* with that purchase. Before long, people in town were calling it the Bradley Funeral Home. But officially it was McCandless, Zobel & Bradley.

Dad kept those original names in it as long as he owned the business—nearly forty years. McCandless & Zobel meant something to the history of the town, to its memory of itself. That was more important to John Bradley than advancing his own name.

Dad bought the funeral home along about my first birthday, in February 1955. I was the fourth of the eight Bradley kids. Before me there were Kathy, Steve, and Mark. Afterward we were joined by Barbara, Patrick, Joe, and Tom.

The funeral home was a large corner property; everyone in town knew where John Bradley could be found. And people sought him out. My dad wasn't an embalmer; he had assistants who did that. He was a diplomat. He was a psychiatrist, a psychologist, a counselor. If you lived around Antigo and your father died, you called John. If you had a problem with the Social

Security Administration, John would help you with that. You didn't know how you were going to pay that doctor bill? John Bradley would have a plan.

Just as he'd cared about his fellow Marines, John Bradley cared about the people of his town, their struggles and triumphs, their opinions. And the people sensed his caring.

In the same spirit of service, my dad was president of just about everything: the school board, the PTA, the Lions, the Elks. His leadership and service were standards that were not lost on me or my siblings. In grade school and high school the morning announcements were often read by a Bradley. The spokesperson for the school was a Bradley. I was president of my class for six, seven years in a row.

Dad's actions always spoke louder than words. They spoke so loudly, in fact, that the words we all wanted to hear never broke the surface: the words that would explain to us what the war and Iwo Jima had been like for him.

For decades—for an entire generation—those words remained unspoken. And so they grew unimportant, at least most of the time. Neither I nor my brothers or sisters read a single book about Iwo Jima while my father was alive. How could we be so incurious? The answer, I think, lies in the attitude of unimportance my father projected. The subject of the flag raising, for him, was to be avoided at all costs.

And so it was only outsiders, strangers, who brought the subject up with him—mostly reporters who phoned once a year, in early February, near the anniversary of the flag raising. Dad never took the calls, and he enlisted our help in protecting him. We were trained to tell reporters that John Bradley was "unavailable, fishing in Canada."

My father never went fishing in Canada. Often he was sitting across the table from us as we gave this excuse. I don't remember him ever telling us why he did not want to take the calls. And we never questioned him.

My father was a man firmly anchored to the world of real things, real values. The photograph represented something private to him, something he could never put into words. It didn't represent any abstraction such as "valor" or "the American fighting spirit." Probably it represented Mike, Harlon, Ira, Franklin, Rene, and the other boys who fought alongside him on Iwo Jima, boys whose lives he'd saved or tried to save.

After John Bradley's death, when I began my search for his past, I asked my mother to tell me everything he had ever said to her about Iwo Jima.

"Well," she answered, "that won't take long. He only spoke of Iwo Jima once, on our first date. I was probing him for details, and he spoke for seven or eight disinterested minutes. All the while he was absentmindedly fingering his silver cigarette lighter. And that was it. The only time he talked about it in our forty-seven-year marriage."

My brother Mark had to ask him about it for a history assignment once. My father's answer was: "We were just there, we put a pole up, and someone snapped a picture." End of interview.

My sister Kathy hit a similar wall when she asked Dad to speak about Iwo Jima to her grade-school class. "Dad looked down, cast his eyes away, shook his head in the negative, but didn't say anything," she recalls. "I went to Mom and asked her about it and she said, 'Your father feels the real heroes are the men who died on Iwo Jima.' "

Why did he almost never speak of his past, and then only painfully, between long, excruciating silences? Several answers come to mind.

The media is one. For good reason, Dad distrusted journalists. He'd seen how frequently reporters embellished the interviews he'd given shortly after coming home and on the bond tour. And reporters never got the heart of it right. The real story, as Dad saw it, was simple and unadorned: A flag needed to be replaced. The pole was heavy. The sun was just right. A chance shot turned an unremarkable act into a remarkable photograph.

There were other plausible reasons for Dad's silence. Iggy, for example—the pain and anger of remembering what had happened to Iggy, and of the visit Doc had made to Iggy's parents after the war.

Another answer may have been as uncomplicated, as unmysterious, as John Bradley himself. I think my father kept his silence for the same reason most men who had seen combat in World War II—or any war—kept silent: because the totality of it was simply too painful for words.

I believe my dad coped by making himself not think about the war, the island, his dead comrades. He coped by getting on with life. He seemed almost to have erased the pain and shock from his memory.

But forgetting had not come easily for John Bradley. He may have spoken about Iwo Jima for only seven or eight minutes to Elizabeth Van Gorp on their first date. But after they were married, my mother told me, he wept at night, in his sleep. He wept in his sleep for four years.

My father did not want to be called a hero. In that misunderstood and corrupted word, I think, lay the final reason for John Bradley's silence. Today the word *hero* has been diminished, confused with *celebrity*. But in my father's generation the word meant something. Celebrities seek fame. They take actions to get attention. But heroes are heroes because they have risked something to help others.

The irony, of course, is that Doc Bradley was indeed a hero on Iwo Jima—many times over. Those moments, however, had nothing to do with the flag raising. When he was shown the photo for the first time, he had no idea what he was looking at. He did not recognize himself or any of the others. The raising of that pole was as forgettable as tying the laces of his boots.

So he knew real heroism. And no matter how many millions of people thought otherwise, he understood that this image of heroism was not the real thing.

FIFTEEN

Coming Home

Nothing except a battle lost can be half so melancholy as a battle won.

—Duke of Wellington

In the spring of 1945, in six pockets of America, six mothers waited for word. They did not yet know one another—or that they were soon to be linked by happenstance and history. To be linked, for a while, with a seventh mother through a painful accident of misidentification.

In Weslaco, Texas, the Blocks had still not received Harlon's March 1 letter reporting that he had "come through without a scratch." But Belle felt secure. She felt an almost mystical connection to her boy because, as she was telling everyone, he was in the famous photograph. She felt just as certain that Harlon was alive.

On a windblown day toward the end of the month a telegram from the commandant of the Marine Corps arrived, telling her and Ed otherwise.

Martha Strank was at home in her New World "palace" at 121 Pine Street, Franklin Borough, Pennsylvania, when the Western Union deliveryman knocked. Two of her sons were on active duty: Mike, on Iwo Jima, and Pete, a sailor aboard the USS *Franklin* in the Pacific. Her young son John later described the way Martha stood in the doorway trying to figure how to deal with the presence of the Western Union man, the piece of yellow paper he held, the bad news she was certain it bore.

"She was so upset that she told the man, 'You open it,' " John recalled. " 'I can't do that,' he responded. 'But I want you to,' she said. She was pleading. He opened it and read it to her. She fainted."

John told me decades later: "Her hair turned white within a couple of months. It had been coal black before Mike died."

Even as grief, born of telegrams, began to flow into households such as the Stranks' and Blocks', a different kind of current—a current of exaltation—gathered its own momentum in the nation. This current was born of the photograph. The photograph seemed to illuminate the air around it; it released pulses of hope and pride and often tears in people who glimpsed it.

There was almost no discussion of the facts surrounding the flag raising. The photo looked heroic, and that was enough. It was certainly enough for the Treasury Department. A two-front world war and the secret and fabulously expensive building of the atomic bomb had drained the national coffers. In the 1940s U.S. government, war expenses were considered outside the normal federal budget. A wartime government was obliged to take its case repeatedly before the citizenry, hoping for a patriotic volunteer response.

War bonds were the chief mechanism for this volunteer funding. Essentially a citizen's loan to the government, purchase of a bond at the issue price of $18.75 gave the government temporary use of the buyer's money; the buyer in turn could expect a yield, in ten years, of $25. The government stimulated these purchases through bond tours. World War II had already produced six of these public fund-raisers, and the American people had dug deeply into their pockets each time. Yet the need to finance the unfinished business against the Japanese—a conflict that still promised bloodshed on a massive scale—meant the Treasury Department could leave nothing to chance. Now the anxious organizers at the Treasury moved to secure the one element that could make the seventh tour shine like no previous one: the presence of living figures from the beloved flag-raising icon.

President Roosevelt's order to find and bring home the surviving flag raisers had so far yielded the identification of only one of the boys, Rene Gagnon. Mike, Franklin, and the misidentified Hank Hansen were dead. Harlon and Ira had not yet been considered, and no one was sure about Doc.

If Ira had his way, no one was going to discover the truth. Ira knew that he was in the photo, and he knew that Rene knew. The intense combat veteran told the teenage errand boy that he didn't want to go on a bond tour and that if Rene revealed that Ira was in the photograph, Ira would kill him.

By concealing his identity, Ira was disobeying President Roosevelt, his commander in chief, but the Pima Indian could think of no other choice. What were these people thinking? The idea of going around the country being congratulated for his presence in a photograph, following a month of witnessing death and incessant killing, did not connect with his Pima modesty and self-effacement.

Whatever Ira's motivation, Rene was not about to challenge the combat veteran. He agreed to keep Ira's secret. In contrast to his comrade in arms, Rene very much was looking forward to his new celebrity. Among the three surviving flag raisers, he would be the first to face the flashbulbs. Doc, his legs peppered with shrapnel, had been evacuated to Guam and now lay convalescing in a hospital in Honolulu. Ira, keeping mum, was still with Easy, on a transport ship bound for Hilo. Rene was on a date with destiny all by himself.

The New Hampshire mill worker landed in Washington on Saturday, April 7. A waiting car rushed him directly to Marine Corps headquarters. In a large conference room furnished with note-taking staff and a blown-up image of the photograph, Marine brass pressed the new hero for the identities of the other flag raisers. As he had done for Keyes Beech, Rene offered five names: Strank, Bradley, Sousley, the misidentified Hansen, and himself.

But the enlarged photo showed six figures. "Who is the sixth man?" the brass pressed.

Rene froze, staring at the photo. Yes, he admitted, it appeared that there were six. Rene's hands began to shake. He knew who it was but had promised not to tell, Rene informed his interrogators. Impossible, they countered; they were all under presidential orders. Slowly, painfully, Rene gave up his secret. Orders were flashed to the Pacific to bring back the sixth man. Ira's days as just another Marine were over.

Meanwhile, a newspaperman from the Manchester *Union-Leader*, alerted by an AP wire story, knocked on Irene Gagnon's front door. Rene's mother cried with relief and joy to learn that her only boy was not only alive, but a hero. The reporter suggested that he drive Irene to Pauline's house for a photo of the hero's mother and girlfriend together. Across the front page of the April 7 *Union-Leader* were splashed two oversized photographs: Rene's formal Marine Corps portrait and a shot of an "electrified" mom and fiancée. Within days Pauline, the textile mill worker, was enjoying a new national nickname: "The Sweetheart of Iwo Jima."

On Sunday, April 8, the Marines released the identification of the six figures as given by Rene. The next day the photo reappeared in newspapers across the country, this time with a name linked by arrow to each flag raiser, save one. The AP copy provided detailed biographies of five of the boys: Hank Hansen, Doc, Ira, Rene, and Mike. Only Franklin, killed on March 21, remained unidentified, pending notification of his mother.

On Monday, April 9, Goldie received the news. Her last name was no longer Sousley. She'd remarried, to a man named Hensley Price. Because Goldie didn't have a phone, a barefoot young boy ran the telegram up to her farm.

The news of Franklin's death spread fast in the Kentucky hills. But it was Goldie's reaction that Hilltop would remember with the greatest sorrow. Goldie, who still put in long days of farmwork, just as she had when Franklin was a little boy. Goldie, who had beamed her radiant smile through all of it and who always had an encouraging word for others. Her freckled son had inherited that smile, and a reminder of it was on display in her living room: a glossy photograph of Franklin in uniform. People who knew her said that Goldie often turned that photograph over to read the words he'd written on the back:

> *To the kindest friend I ever knew,*
> *The one I told all my troubles to.*
> *You can look the world over, but you won't find another*
> *Like you, my dear Mother.*
> *Love,*
> *Franklin*

Fifty-three years later Goldie's sister Florine Moran told me that the neighbors could hear Goldie scream all that night and into the morning. The neighbors lived a quarter-mile away.

In Pennsylvania, the news of Mike Strank's death was followed quickly by the revelation of his place in the iconic image. His brother John remembered: "We were walking home from a memorial service for Mike," he said. "We saw people all around our house. It was mass confusion, with neighbors and local press. I was wondering, 'What's happening?' Then they told us the story had just broken that Mike was in the photo."

Far to the northwest, in rural Wisconsin, Kathryn and Cabbage Bradley's neighbors called with their congratulations. Cabbage basked in his son's fame, but Kathryn—closer to her son in temperament—worried about appearing immodest. Soon she found something else to worry about. When she had learned her Jack was in the photo, she reread some of the recent days' press coverage about the event. She discovered an AP story datelined Pearl Harbor about Rene coming home, which had reported: "There are six men in the historic photo—five Marines and one Navy hospital corpsman." Then the dispatch added the chilling sentence "The Navy man later lost a leg in battle"—yet another error from the media. The Navy man had not lost a leg. He had shrapnel in his leg, but there was no one who said he wouldn't recover.

My father, in fact, was in a Honolulu hospital when he first glimpsed the photograph. Years later he recounted his reaction. "I thought, 'Holy man, is that ever a terrific picture!'" he recalled. "There was a lot of confusion. We weren't sure who the flag raisers were. I couldn't pick myself out. It was such an insignificant thing at the time."

On the same day, April 9, word reached Ira Hayes, on his way to Hilo, that his secret had been exposed. He reached Hilo on April 12. Three days later Ira reluctantly climbed aboard a plane for Marine headquarters in Washington.

In Boston, the newspapers unknowingly began to perpetuate the single most tragic of all the errors about the flag raising. The coverage offered solace—temporary solace, as it proved—to Hank Hansen's grieving mother, Mrs. Joseph Evelley. Mustering a smile, she proudly held the photograph for a reporter to see: "See, see the photograph," Madeline Evelley insisted. "That's my son, with his left hand gripped around the flag's staff. Henry put the American flag up on Iwo Jima."

In Weslaco, Belle Block remained unconvinced by this assertion. When Ed Block Sr. showed the photo to her, with

Hansen's identification attached, she just shook her head. "I don't care what the papers say," she repeated for perhaps the hundredth time. "I know my boy."

Before the flag raisers were known, the photo stood for a great military victory. Now, with names attached, the public began to see in it a manifestation of eternal American values.

At the outset it was Rene who satisfied America's thirst for humanizing details of the flag raisers. It was the lean-faced, dark-browed Manchester boy, his mother and his fiancée at his side, who confirmed the fondest elements of American wartime myth: the fighting hero as the wholesome boy next door, eager for marriage, picket fences, and Mom's cooking.

Now, for the bond tour to come, and for long afterward, Rene's reaction to all the public attention would prove to be just the opposite of my father's attitude. Rene loved the glare of fame. Fame, however, did not necessarily love Rene. His became a life of missed connections, of circumstance turning against him, of perceived bad breaks and broken promises.

On Thursday, April 12, for example, he was told his hometown was going to give him a parade, a hero's welcome. Instead, at the last moment, a news bulletin flashed across the radio airwaves: The president of the United States was dead. Franklin Delano Roosevelt had succumbed to a cerebral hemorrhage at Warm Springs, Georgia. Rene's ride in the open limousine got canceled. The letdown would form a motif for his life: The parade he always sought would never quite get under way.

Jack Bradley slipped back into America without much fanfare. When he arrived in Bethesda he called home, speaking with his parents for the first time in months. He talked matter-of-factly of his wounds and of how he had been brought back to Washington by presidential order. After the conversation Kathryn was strangely sad. For a long time she kept the reason to herself: She thought her son was trying not to hurt her feelings by speaking of the leg he had lost.

In Wisconsin the state senate passed a resolution on April 12, praising "John Bradley" as one who "helped plant the American flag on Mount Suribachi." Doc was the nickname he would soon put aside, along with his wartime mementos. Jack he would still remain to his family and his Wisconsin friends; but it was as John he'd be introduced to all who met him from now on.

On Thursday, April 19, the final living flag raiser touched down in Washington. Ira arrived to find Rene, down from New Hampshire, and John, over from Bethesda on his crutches, awaiting him. Up to now the three had been serving the War Department. But now, by presidential order, their services were transferred to the Treasury Department in a new battle, this one for money. And the Treasury Department did not believe in a gradual start: On the following day the three were to meet the new president, Harry Truman, in the White House.

During Ira's initial briefing at the Marine barracks, he was shown the enlarged photograph of the flag raising. Ira spotted the error of identification immediately. The figure at the base of the pole was not Hank Hansen; it was Harlon Block. Ira remembered what Rene Gagnon and John Bradley could not have remembered, because they did not join the little cluster until the last moment: that it was Harlon, Mike, Franklin, and himself who had ascended Suribachi at midmorning to lay telephone wire; it was Rene who had come along with the replacement flag. Hansen had not been a part of this action.

Ira acted on his first impulse, which was to set the record straight. He pointed out the error to the Marine public relations officer who'd been assigned to keep an eye on the young Pima. The officer's response stunned Ira: He was ordered to keep his mouth shut, since the report had already been released and it was too late to do anything.

Ira was ill at ease upon his reunion with Rene. He did not kill his former Easy Company mate, as he had sworn to do, but he didn't forgive him for snitching, either. He gave the younger boy the silent treatment, speaking to him only through my father. The American public never glimpsed this rift. To the crowds, the boys were like the Three Musketeers, except they had a different collective name—sometimes they were the "Iwo Jima flag-raising heroes," but usually they were simply "the heroes."

It must have felt surreal to the boys. Heroes? As Ira would write in wonderment to his parents: "It's funny what a picture can do."

The first day of the three boys' official "heroism" began early, at 9:15 A.M., in the Oval Office. The new president greeted them enthusiastically. The boys presented Mr. Truman with a copy of the official bond tour poster in a gold frame. Truman, smiling, thanked them for the important duty they were about to perform for their country. He grasped John's hand and then Rene's. Then he turned to Ira and said, "You are a true American because you are an American Indian. And now, son, you are a true American hero."

As the three survivors came to terms with their unreal celebrity, in Weslaco the Blocks were finally coming to terms with Harlon's very real death. Belle had finally admitted to herself that Harlon wouldn't be coming home. But she was as insistent about Harlon's rightful place in the photograph as Ira was desirous of escaping his.

Belle's husband, Ed senior, was imprisoned inside his stoic German grief. Ed didn't cry, didn't express his grief in words. But the boy who had become practically his best friend, whose gridiron exploits were a constant source of joy, was gone, and for Ed, the pain must have been excruciating.

But life had to go on: the lives of the survivors, the life of the nation. The grieving Ed Block could never have imagined the great burden that Harlon's three comrades carried with them as they prepared for the marathon bond tour. Quite likely the boys themselves did not fully imagine it.

Others did, however. At the end of the boys' meeting with Harry Truman, Treasury secretary Morgenthau lingered with the new president just long enough to present him with some dire numbers. The war had now devoured $88 billion out of a fiscal year budget of $99 billion. But government revenue totaled only $46 billion. It was critical that the bond tour bring in some big numbers.

SIXTEEN

The Bond Tour

It's funny what a picture can do.

—Ira Hayes

Fourteen billion dollars, to be exact. That was the monetary goal set by the Treasury Department for the seventh bond tour: Fourteen billion to keep feeding, clothing, sheltering, and arming the millions of men and women still fighting World War II and to provide more planes, ships, and tanks for their effort. Fourteen billion: a mountain of money that must have seemed as formidable, in its own way, as Suribachi.

And now the three surviving flag raisers would lead the charge to take that mountain.

As the bond tour moved toward its May 9 kickoff in Washington—it would storm through thirty-three cities before winding up back in the nation's capital on July 4—the photograph's mystical hold on the nation continued to deepen. Detached from the real circumstances that produced it, the photograph had become a receptacle for America's emotions, standing for everything good that Americans wanted it to stand for.

An entrepreneur offered the Associated Press $200,000 for the rights to the photo. A congressman, W. Sterling Cole of New York, declared that it should become "public property"— it meant too much to the nation to be used for mere commerce. The AP finally decided to donate the rights to the photo to the government, with royalties going to a sailors' retirement fund.

The sculptor Felix de Weldon went to work on a larger model of his flag-raising monument. And in Times Square in New York City, the crossroads of the world, a five-story flag-raising statue was being installed.

On Tuesday, May 8, the newspapers trumpeted the biggest news yet in the war: Germany had surrendered. And still a development regarding the photograph worked its way onto the front page of the *New York Times:* Joe Rosenthal had won a Pulitzer prize for being at the right place at the right time.

Bright sunshine and soft breezes graced the bond tour's opening ceremonies in Washington the next day. As military brass glittered and flags flapped in the breeze, members of the president's cabinet and of both houses of Congress assembled outside the Capitol to wish the tour Godspeed. Within a few hours Ira, Rene, and John made their first stop—Grand Central Station in New York City. They gaped at blowups of the bond tour poster that papered the terminal's cavernous main hall. Whisked ten blocks up Park Avenue to the luxurious Waldorf-Astoria, the flag raisers passed likenesses of themselves that seemed to cover just about every surface in the city. New York City's bond sales goal was $287 million, and the boys' schedule was crammed. They began Thursday morning with an autograph-signing session at the Roxy Theater in Times Square, and ended their city stay on Friday with Mayor Fiorello La Guardia's unveiling of the five-story Iwo Jima statue in front of tens of thousands of enthralled New Yorkers. The *Times* coverage the next day featured a photograph of John raising the flag over the statue as Rene, Ira, Marine Corps commandant Alexander Vandegrift, and the mayor saluted.

Again and again, despite abundant opportunity, the three boys refused to pick up the theme of press and speech makers and portray themselves as valiant warriors who hoisted the colors against enemy fire. Clearly, modesty wasn't enough for the aggressive press. Glory was the thing that sold papers. It was my father who finally cut the reporters off at one press conference. They should just report the truth, John Bradley said: "It took everyone on that island and the men on the ships offshore to get the flag up on Suribachi."

After the first day's activities, Ira learned to take refuge from such ordeals at local bars. The three flag raisers were officially chaperoned on the bond tour by Keyes Beech, the Marine correspondent who first queried Rene about the identities of the six men. Beech's job was to make travel arrangements and keep an eye on the boys. However, as conscientious as Beech tried to be, it was impossible to keep Ira in line. If Ira wanted to get drunk, he usually found a way—then suffered through the next morning. Ira was a good fighting man, but he wasn't the kind of guy you'd pick to send on a bond tour.

On Saturday cheering crowds in Philadelphia got a glimpse of the boys as their motorcade sped to Independence Hall, where they posed for the cameras in front of the Liberty Bell.

The next stop was Boston. A torrential downpour did not keep two hundred thousand Bostonians from lining the parade route to applaud the heroes. On Boston Common, speaker after speaker spoke of the boys' gallantry.

On Monday afternoon, May 14, the flag raisers rolled back into New York for ceremonies that would spotlight a dramatic Wall Street war-bond pledge. Joining Ira, John, and Rene on the speakers' platforms would be the mothers of the three fallen flag raisers. John Strank escorted his mother, Martha, from Franklin Borough, Pennsylvania, to the city. "My dad was just so broken up after Mike's death that he couldn't go," John recalled. "It was a challenge for my mother. She worried that her English was not good enough." From Hilltop, Kentucky, Goldie arrived and must have been overwhelmed with crowds. She'd never before been more than 150 miles from home, she told a reporter. From Somerville, Massachusetts, Mrs. Madeline Evelley, the mother of Hank Hansen, still identified as the sixth flag raiser, traveled to the city with her daughter Gertrude.

Everyone checked in at the Waldorf, where politicians, celebrities, and military brass doted on the boys. But for Ira, John, and Rene, the people who mattered were the three bereaved mothers. "I remember Ira Hayes grabbing my mother; he was so emotional, he wouldn't let her go," said John Strank. "He was sobbing."

My father and Mrs. Evelley gravitated toward each other. John had been Hank's close friend. He had rushed to Hansen when he was shot and had tried to save his life. And now, here in the glitter of a far different world, John at last was able to make the quiet gesture he had pledged to make amid the smoke and slaughter of Iwo Jima: He withdrew from his pocket the watch that he had slipped from dead Hank's wrist, and placed it in Madeline's hands.

The next morning the mothers and the boys were ushered onto a reviewing balcony at the New York Stock Exchange. Trading was halted as the ticker sign flashed WELCOME IWO JIMA HEROES and the traders erupted in applause. Minutes later the president of the New York Stock Exchange stunned the crowd with an announcement: The Wall Street broker-dealer syndicate had pledged to raise $1 billion for the bond drive— enough to finance creation of a fleet of sixteen hundred B-29 Superfortress bombers, geared to the destruction of Japan.

For the six guests on the platform—the three flag raisers and the three bereaved mothers—this moment must have throbbed with competing emotions. The boys, so recently returned from battle, had not yet recovered from its ravages. My father was crying in his sleep. Ira was drinking hard. And Rene had developed a tic that would never go away. Yet here they were, the inspirations for an outpouring of wealth that might save thousands of American lives.

If the boys were a bit dazed, the three mothers were still in a haze of grief. From the families of the three, I have often heard the remark that their grief could never end: The fact of the photograph obliged them to relive it over and over.

On Saturday, May 19, a hundred thousand cheering people crammed themselves into Chicago's Loop to greet the flag raisers. Humphrey Bogart was in town, and Lauren Bacall, and Ida Lupino.

Responding to the welcome from city officials, my young father stepped to the microphone and repeated the message he had delivered in other cities: "Men of the fighting fronts cannot understand the need for rallies to sell bonds for purchase of seriously needed supplies. The bond buyer is asked only to lend his money at a profit. The fighting man is asked to give his life."

The crowd dug deep into its pockets.

Sunday was "I Am an American Day," sponsored by the Hearst newspapers. At Soldier Field, Hearst had financed the construction of a miniature Suribachi to promote the right atmosphere. But as fifty thousand people poured into the football stadium to see the replica and to hear the three flag raisers, something was not quite right.

The previous night, police had found Ira Hayes walking the streets, drunk. Beech and others hauled him back to the hotel, poured ice water over him, and "slapped him into something resembling sobriety." By this time the flag raising at Soldier Field was only an hour away.

For the triumphal tour around the stadium in an open Cadillac, Beech made sure to wedge Ira between John and Rene so that he would not fall out. Observing all this from the reviewing stand was Marine commandant Vandegrift. Reports had reached the commandant that "the Indian" was creating a bad name for himself and the Corps. Something, it was clear, would have to be done about Ira Hayes.

The Pima Indian wobbled through the flag-raising reenactment, joining John and Rene in hoisting the famous flag. And then Ira Hayes packed his bags and, with the others, made ready to hit the road again.

· · ·

After several days in Detroit and Indianapolis, the tour returned to Chicago. Late that morning a Marine colonel telephoned Keyes Beech with an order to bring Ira Hayes to his office. There, the young Pima faced the bad news: he was to rejoin his unit, Easy Company, in the Pacific. The order had come from Commandant Vandegrift. Ira was denied a furlough to see his family in Arizona, but he was given a face-saving cover, one that ironically confirmed his press image as a fighting man who yearned for active duty: He was being sent back overseas "at his own request."

The next morning, as Rene, John, and Keyes Beech headed for St. Louis, Ira stopped off in San Francisco and wrote a letter home. Revealing in a way that few of his "tough guy" statements to the press were, it showed the embarrassment, hurt pride, and frustrated yearning of a still young, still tender, and deeply wounded man:

Dear Parents & Brothers;

This may shock you but do not be afraid. At the present I'm in San Francisco just got in this morning from Chicago. And leaving this morning for Pearl Harbor. There's supposed to be some show out there that's why Gen. Rockey wants me back there just for it. Then back here again to rejoin Gagnon, Bradley and Beech. So do not worry. Today Bradley & the others are in St. Louis and I sure wish I was with them. But that has to wait till later. Well I'll close here as I have a few things I'd like to do. God Bless all of you & please for my sake do not worry.

Your Loving Son & Bro.
I.H.H.

The "show" that Ira referred to was nothing less than the contemplated invasion of Japan. Ira would travel some four thousand miles west to rejoin Easy Company in Hawaii, where the Fifth Division was training for the invasion.

St. Louis, Tulsa, San Antonio, Austin, Portland, Seattle—for Jack and Rene, the cities began to blur. So did the public's adulation, the questions from the press, and the boys' persistent disclaimers about being heroes. None of it really registered with the public or the media. The photograph had transported many thousands of anxious, grieving, and war-weary Americans into a radiant state of mind where faith, patriotism, mythic history, and the simple capacity to hope all lived together.

Appleton, El Paso, Houston, Dallas, Phoenix, Tucson, Denver, Milwaukee, Atlanta, Greensboro, Tampa, Columbia, Charleston, Richmond, Norfolk. As the tour headed south, the summer weather turned hot, and fatigue and numbness overtook John and Rene. It was all train stations, airports, flashbulbs, adoring faces, unfamiliar beds, no sleep, the same old questions. Luxury was no longer a sumptuous banquet, a well-appointed suite. Luxury was a good shave, a hot bath, a square meal.

Despite their weariness with the tour as it neared the final phase of its eight-week loop around America, John and Rene must have had some sense of what they had accomplished. The bond tour was exceeding all expectations. With the invasion of Okinawa now commanding the headlines and patriotic fervor running high, the tour was inspiring subscriptions at a rate that would astound the nation when they were finally totaled.

The bond tour revenues would have immediate use. America was pouring every resource into the Pacific war. At the beginning of June President Truman had announced doubling to seven million the troops pitted against Japan—higher than the U.S. deployment in Europe at its peak. All strategies pointed to an invasion of the Japanese home islands.

On June 18 Truman's military advisers presented the president with horrifying projections: Up to 35 percent—nearly 270,000—of these men would be killed or wounded in the first thirty days of fighting. After 120 days, the time allotted for occupying the island, U.S. casualties could reach 395,000.

That was only the first wave of men. The second—an invasion of Honshu and the capture of Tokyo, projected for March 1946—would require a force of one million. And that push would exact hundreds of thousands of casualties.

On the night of July 4 the sky of the nation's capital was ablaze with fireworks as some 350,000 spectators—a larger crowd even than would assemble for Martin Luther King Jr.'s March on Washington eighteen years later—sat around the Mall and basked in the glow of patriotism. The seventh bond tour had completed its triumphal circuit of the nation and come back home to Washington.

The next day Rene Gagnon reported to Marine headquarters. He was given a short leave before his transfer back to San Diego. On July 7 he married Pauline Harnois in Baltimore, with John Bradley serving as best man. Pauline accompanied Rene as far west as Pasadena. By November 7, he was on active duty in Tsingtao, China.

At the end of the summer the final totals for the bond tour were in. The tour had not just met its goal, but nearly doubled it: Americans had pledged $26.3 billion. This was equal to almost half of the 1946 total U.S. government budget of $56 billion.

An Iwo Jima commemorative stamp was issued on July 11, the anniversary of the founding of the Marine Corps Reserve. It was the first stamp to feature living people. Even presidents had to die to get their image on a stamp. It immediately broke post office records for first-day sales, topping 400,000. In time 150 million stamps would be printed, making it the best-selling stamp in history up to that point.

John Bradley, again being treated at nearby Bethesda for his wounds, sat quietly among the dignitaries—the only one of the six figures present—during the Washington ceremonies that opened the sale of the stamp. He listened as the postmaster proclaimed: "We honor the individuals here depicted, who by God's mercy still live among us. But they are not represented on this stamp as individuals. In the glorious tradition of the Marine Corps, they submerged their identities, giving themselves wholly to the United States of America."

I can only imagine the thoughts that must have coursed through my father's mind as he heard these words: my father, age twenty-one, two years out of his adolescence, who had never wished more fervently for anything than he wished for the day he could return to Wisconsin, marry, start a family, and open his funeral home; who had held on to this quiet dream through the long months in the Pacific; ~~who indeed~~ "gave himself wholly to the United States of America."

My father was now listening to the news that his identity would never again be his own, that it would remain, in some irretrievable way, the property of the nation. He would not be able to leave the image. The image would not leave him. Like it or not, he would always be a figure in the photograph.

SEVENTEEN

A Conflict of Honor

That's Harlon. I know my boy.

—Belle Block

In Weslaco, Texas, at about the time the bond tour was looping back east for its triumphal finale, Ed and Belle Block were packing their belongings for a private journey west. They were moving to California—to Loma Linda, where the Seventh-Day Adventist Church had a large presence.

Loma Linda was Belle's idea. In fact, she'd insisted on it. Belle had never adjusted to farm living in south Texas. For Ed, the farm was the life he knew in his bones. But he did not resist his wife's strong desire to leave.

Sorrow and solitude had steered the Blocks' marriage into trouble. The stresses had begun even before they had learned of Harlon's death. They had already sold their house when the telegram arrived. But the bad news had only hardened Belle's determination. "Harlon's death exploded Mom from the Valley," daughter Maurine later recalled. "She couldn't go on; there was just too much hurt. She used to say, 'Everything bad that ever happened to me happened in the Valley.'"

In June 1945, while the nation celebrated the grand tour of the surviving flag raisers and their patriotic show, Ed and Belle quietly loaded up their car and, with their young sons Mel, Larry, and Corky, left Weslaco, Texas, for California.

Loma Linda did indeed bring Belle some measure of peace. The family bought a small house, and Belle busied herself with church life and her children while Ed scouted for farmland. Belle's fixation on Harlon's place in the photograph, though, remained unshakable. In fact, it grew stronger. One of the first items she unpacked in their new dwelling was a copy of the photo.

California was less welcoming to Ed. It proved as bad a fit for him as Texas had for Belle. He could not believe the price of land here; it dwarfed his small nest egg. A stranger to the local banks, he was unable to secure a loan. The dream of a farm began to wither. Frustrated and miserable, he told Belle one day: "I've got to make us a living. I'm going back to Texas."

Whatever hopes he might have harbored about staying together with Belle were dashed when she replied: "Go. But I'm not." Ed picked up a used Model A, threw his luggage into it, and hit the long road back to the Valley.

In late July the leaders of the "big three" Allied nations—Winston Churchill of Great Britain, Harry Truman of the United States, and Josef Stalin of the Soviet Union—met in Potsdam, Germany, to map out the closure of the Pacific war.

Clearly, the fanatical Japanese war machine would capitulate only to direct force. That meant an invasion of staggering proportions: I.5 million combat troops committed to the initial assault waves, with reserves bringing the total to 4.5 million. The projected casualties beggared the imagination: a million Americans, half a million British.

Churchill, Truman, and their aides conferred discreetly on one further, just-emerging alternative. Days earlier, on July 16, thousands of miles away on Alamogordo Air Base in New Mexico, the first atom bomb had been successfully tested. On July 26 the Allied leaders issued their Potsdam Declaration: Japan must surrender or face "utter and complete destruction." Japan ignored the ultimatum. It still had 2.5 million active troops and a civilian population that could be mustered into a suicide defense force. "One hundred million hearts beating as one" was the Japanese slogan. The Land of the Rising Sun would fight to the last *issen gorin*.

Through the summer of 1945 Iwo Jima continued to serve the purpose for which it had been wrested from the Japanese: to provide air cover and an emergency landing strip for the B-29 bombers flying from their base in Tinian to their targets in Japan.

In the dim predawn light of August 6, 1945, passing over Iwo Jima, the pilot of one of those bombers was joined by two other B-29s. At 6:07 the three bombers dipped their wings in a salute to Mike, Harlon, Franklin, and the thousands of other boys buried below.

The pilot's name was Paul Tibbets. Secured in his jacket were twelve cyanide tablets, one for each crew member in case they were shot down. They were on a mission whose secrets were too vital to be divulged under Japanese torture.

The name of Tibbets's B-29 was the *Enola Gay*. His payload was a single weapon, nicknamed "Little Boy." It was a code name for the first atomic bomb to be used in war. The target was the Japanese city of Hiroshima.

John Bradley spent the last half of July and part of September at Bethesda Naval Medical Center, undergoing treatment for his legs that had been delayed by the bond tour. In mid-September he was given a leave, and he hurried off to Appleton.

A day or so later Betty Van Gorp was out on a date at a dance club. "Jack came in with some other guys and sat in the same booth with us," my mother told me. "We hadn't seen each other for years, and we caught up. My date didn't dance, so Jack asked me to dance."

A couple of weeks after that, Betty saw Jack again. He showed up with another male friend of hers at the courthouse, where Betty was employed as a social worker. They chatted, and the two men left. Not too many minutes after that, Betty's work phone rang. It was Jack. He wanted to take her out to dinner the next night.

"Over dinner I asked him about the flag raising," my mother said. This was the night he spoke to her about Iwo Jima—for the first and last time. "He told it like he must have told it many times: like a speech, nothing personal, just the facts."

Later they went to a dance club and chatted with high school friends. On the following night they took in a movie. Betty's impression of Jack, she recalled, was that he was mature, that he had been through a lot, and that his responsibilities for people's lives had required him to make important, snap decisions far beyond his young age.

Not long after that, Jack was holding Betty tightly in his arms and telling her, "I love you with my whole heart and soul." Betty was touched by the way Jack said the words "heart and soul." No one had ever said that to her. "I knew he really loved me," she said.

John left the next day for more surgery on his shrapnel wounds at Bethesda. When his surgery was complete, he left to meet his final public obligation as a figure in the photograph. November 10, 1945, marked the 170th anniversary of the Marine Corps, and John participated in festivities with the Marine brass.

Three days later he was discharged. He was twenty-two and had spent thirty-four months, a seventh of his life, in the Navy—the outfit he'd joined so that he would not have to fight on land.

He made straight for Appleton, and he and Betty were engaged on December 3. In January 1946 he began classes in the Wisconsin Institute of Mortuary Science, in Milwaukee, while working part time at the Weiss Funeral Home there. The life he had dreamed of in California, in Hawaii, on the sulfur island, was finally becoming a reality.

Servicemen's weddings were commonplace events in the spring of 1946, but on Sunday, May 5, a photograph of one of them made newspapers across America. Its caption read: "One of the flag raisers on Iwo Jima, John H. Bradley of Appleton, Saturday married a hometown sweetheart, the former Elizabeth Van Gorp, in St. Mary's Catholic Church there."

After a honeymoon night, John began working full time at

the Fass Funeral Home. Reporters, authors, and collectors of memorabilia tracked him down, but the young husband took his stand early. "It was either a matter of granting interviews full time or trying to make a living for my family," he remarked in a rare interview. "So I decided to make a living for my family and treat everyone the same: no interviews for anyone."

From the earliest days of their marriage John and Betty made a ritual of saying their nightly prayers silently together. It was one of life's small but important gestures that brought them closer to each other. John's other nightly habit, though, kept them slightly apart. When Betty would ask him about it in the morning, my father refused to talk about it. "He'd be sleeping, his eyes closed," was the way my mother remembered it. "But he'd be whimpering. His body would shake, and tears would stream out of his eyes, down his face."

On October 25, 1945, Ira boarded a ship home from Japan. He had been part of the Allied forces who briefly occupied Japan after its formal surrender, which occurred shortly after the United States dropped its second atom bomb, nicknamed "Fat Man," on the Japanese city of Nagasaki.

Ira landed at San Francisco on November 9 and was discharged from active duty at San Diego on December 1, 1945. Just turned twenty-two, he had spent thirty-nine months of his life as a Marine, twenty-three of them in three overseas tours.

Pete Strank, one of Mike's two younger brothers and a Navy man, came home, too, in a sense. Pete had resembled Mike: big at six foot four, boisterous, handsome with a white-toothed smile, full of life. That had changed on March 19, 1945, when Pete's ship, the USS *Franklin*, sixty miles off the coast of Japan, took a hit by a kamikaze dive-bomber.

The *Franklin*, loaded with fully fueled and armed fighter planes, became a bomb herself, a thirty-thousand-ton floating bomb. She burst into an inferno of ignited gasoline. No one thought the *Franklin* would survive. But she did, a husk of her former self, as she limped back to the United States as the most heavily damaged warship in U.S. naval history, her crew the most decorated.

Pete survived in a similar way—a husk of his former self. John Strank, the third brother, told me: "I lost two brothers in the Pacific war."

Rene returned from China in April 1946. Unlike my father or Ira, he came home with hopes of benefiting from his "hero" label. He had a dream of becoming a state police officer and thought he could do it with "connections." But Rene did not meet the qualifications for the job, and no one in the New Hampshire state police seemed inclined to give him a courtesy appointment based on his reputation. Soon Rene was back at work with Pauline in the Manchester mills.

Ira resumed his life at the Pima reservation south of Phoenix, moving back into his family's adobe house. Nancy kept a print of the flag-raising photograph on the wall, but Ira did not encourage conversation about it.

He found menial jobs, day-labor work, mostly near Phoenix. Eventually he bought a dwelling of his own: a room in an abandoned barracks. If Ira thought he could come all the way back to his former life—if he thought the hoopla over the flag-raising photograph would die down now that the war was ended—he was wrong.

"Tourists would drive all over the reservation looking for me," he would later tell a reporter. "They'd spot me in the field, rush up to me with their cameras and ask, 'Are you that Indian that raised the flag on Iwo Jima?' "

Inevitably, perhaps, Ira turned again to the numbing relief that he had sought during the bond tour. As his drinking continued, his face grew heavy and his features thickened. The drunk-and-disorderly arrests piled up. No one on the Pima reservation tried to intervene in his troubles; it was not their way. Then one day in May of 1946 Ira did something that, in my eyes, really did make him a hero. Without telling anyone, he walked off the Gila River reservation and out to the Pearl Harbor Highway, and thumbed his way south toward Tucson.

At Tucson he headed east through Arizona, then New Mexico. He would have ridden in the backs of farm trucks, in the cabs of big rigs, alongside any driver who would pick up an Indian. He would never have told anyone his name.

Crossing the Texas border north of El Paso, he would have passed within seventy-five miles of Alamogordo, where the first atom bomb was tested.

At San Antonio Ira would have headed toward the knife-blade tip of Texas, where the Rio Grande empties into the Gulf of Mexico—toward the Rio Grande Valley and the little towns scattered across it.

At Weslaco Ira would have asked around about Ed Block Sr. No one would have paid much attention to his questions; Ira could have been another laborer looking for work on Ed's cotton farm.

Ira had hitchhiked more than thirteen hundred miles in three days. Now he moved back north out of Weslaco for a few miles, then walked west off the main road until finally, miles later, he could see Ed's cinder-block house.

He walked up the driveway and knocked on the door. No one answered. Ira turned his gaze to the cotton field, where a lone figure was bent over in the hot sun. Ira knew all about cotton fields. He approached the figure silently, from behind. When he was near him he softly asked: "Are you Mr. Block? Harlon's father?"

Many years later Rebecca Salazar—who became Ed's second wife—still remembered the excitement in Ed's voice when he reached her by telephone. "He was almost breathless," Rebecca recalled. "He asked me, 'Do you know that Indian in the flag-raising photo?' I said, 'Yes . . .' And Ed went on, 'Well, he was here today! He just left. He just walked up and started talking to me about Harlon, how they were good friends. He talked about Harlon playing football, about driving the oil trucks with me. He knew everything! He and Harlon had been good buddies.' "

Apparently the conversation out in the cotton field did not last long. As Ed told Rebecca, "Once he knew that I knew

Harlon was in the photo, he just said, 'Okay, well, I guess I'll be off.' We shook hands, and he walked out of the field."

When Ed called his estranged wife in California, Belle was matter-of-fact about the news. She wrote to Ira for confirmation and received a handwritten note telling her what he had told Ed: Harlon was definitely one of the flag raisers.

Belle—haunted Belle, tireless, fixated, unyielding Belle—had been right all along.

On August 16, 1946—the first anniversary of the victory over Japan—the city fathers of Buffalo, New York, invited the three surviving flag raisers to participate in a day of patriotic ceremonies. John declined. Ira and Rene accepted. But if they expected to relive some of the euphoria of the bond tour, they were mistaken.

A photograph in *The New York Times* told it all: There they were, Ira and Rene, raising Old Glory one more time, but there was something forlorn in their attitude.

Rene was particularly full of self-pity. He told the *Times* reporter, "I had no success in my attempt to obtain a police or fire department job in Manchester. I can't find a place to live in my own town. I have to live with my wife's relatives in Hooksett, about eight miles away."

No evidence exists that Rene had sought out the training that would have made him eligible for such jobs. Clearly, this youngest and most naive flag raiser—he was still only twenty-one in 1946—had assumed that being a "hero" entitled him to a kind of appointment for life, complete with compensation.

Meanwhile Ira was telling reporters a slightly different tale of woe: "I want to be out on my own, but out in Arizona the white race looks down on the Indian as if he were a little man and I don't stand a chance anywhere off the reservation unless I come East."

Ira's next remarks perhaps touched the true source of his torment: "Most of our buddies are gone. Three of the men who raised the flag are gone. We hit the beach on Iwo with 250 men and left with 27 a month and a half later. I still think about that all the time."

But even as Ira continued to brood, the seeds of his most singular act of heroism were beginning to bear fruit. His twenty-six-hundred-mile hitchhiking odyssey of the previous spring, from the Gila River reservation in Arizona to Ed Block's south Texas cotton field and back—had put in motion a series of events that quickly reached the highest levels of the U.S. Marine command.

Belle composed a letter to the congressman from the Weslaco district, telling him what Ira Hayes had told Ed and her.

The congressman forwarded Belle's letter to Commandant Vandegrift, who dispatched an aide to the Pima reservation to take Ira's deposition. Ira confirmed in writing what he already told Ed and Belle. He also showed the aide photographs of Hansen on the flag-raising day wearing a different hat and pair of boots than the Marine placing the pole in the ground. *That* figure was Harlon Block, Ira declared.

The Marine Corps sent Ira's deposition along with the photographs to John and to Rene. Both affirmed that the figure in question was not Hank Hansen and that it probably was Harlon Block.

On January 15, 1947, almost two years after the photo

appeared, Commandant Vandegrift mailed a two-page letter addressed to "Mr. and Mrs. Block." He confirmed that a mistake had been made: Henry Hansen was not in the photograph. On the evidence and by consensus, the Marine thrusting the pole into Mount Suribachi was Harlon Block. Belle had finally been vindicated. With nothing more than the rear view of a figure in a wirephoto from six thousand miles away, she had instantly recognized her son.

EIGHTEEN

Movies and Monuments

If everything isn't black and white, I say,
"Why the hell not?"

—John Wayne

In 1947, the year the cold war began, the nation still looked to the figures in the photograph. In February, on the second anniversary of the flag raising, wire-service photographs went out showing John in a suit, arranging flowers in a funeral home; Ira as an Arizona farmer in an open-necked work shirt; Rene in an undershirt, working in the hot Chicopee mill. When John graduated from the Wisconsin mortuary school, when Rene junior was born in Manchester, when Kathleen Bradley was born in Milwaukee, when John found a job in his birth town of Antigo — when all these things happened, the media flashbulbs popped.

Ira continued to make headlines of a darker kind. His arrests for drunkenness in Phoenix and surrounding towns increased. It was not the constant trickle of pestering tourists or reporters coming to his reservation that plagued him as much as it was the comments of his immediate neighbors. The other young Pimas, when they broke their usual stoicism, liked to rib Ira in the wry, almost mocking style that flavored their culture's humor. "Iwo Jima hero!" was their salutation. No phrase in the English language could have been more painful to Ira. Ira didn't seek fame at all. Celebrity found him and wouldn't let go.

Ira was hardly alone in facing his demons. Betty Bradley learned to cope with John's nocturnal weeping. But she was still taken aback one day when, tidying up the contents of John's dresser, she discovered a large knife in one of the drawers. "I asked him why he had it, and he just said, 'Oh, I don't know,' " my mother remembers. "He wasn't a hunter; he had no use for that knife other than for protection."

In January of 1947 the U.S. government began the long process of transporting the bodies of the Marines on Iwo Jima back home. Franklin Runyon Sousley's remains were returned to his mountaintop community in Kentucky. It must have been some comfort to Goldie that the boy who had promised that he would come back a hero was treated like one. Franklin was buried on May 8, 1947, with full honors in the small Elizaville cemetery on a sunny, breezy Saturday before family, friends, townspeople, and dignitaries.

In the fall of the same year Belle Block returned to the Valley—but not to reunite with Ed. She came to witness the burial, in the Weslaco city cemetery, of Harlon. She had driven from California with her sons Mel and Larry. With Ed at their side, they joined a crowd of nearly twenty thousand that had gathered on a hot, windless day to watch the caisson bear Harlon's flag-draped coffin along Texas Avenue.

Behind the caisson walked more than one hundred veterans, followed in turn by their families and friends in cars. Holding the reins of the horses that pulled the caisson, and walking on both its sides, were Harlon's fellow Panthers: surviving members of the undefeated football team he'd played on, the boys who had enlisted together almost five years earlier.

Ed and Belle were civil toward each other that day, but when the ceremonies were over, Belle got in the car and she and her children drove back to California. Belle never returned to the Valley.

Mike Strank was buried at Arlington National Cemetery, joining other fallen heroes and fighting men and women who had selflessly served their country in time of war. It was a fitting place, maybe the only place, for the young man known universally as a "Marine's Marine." A busload of Mike's family and friends came down from Franklin Borough for the occasion.

Ralph "Iggy" Ignatowski's remains were put into the earth of the national military cemetery in Rock Island, Illinois. Like most mothers of dead servicemen, Frances Ignatowski wanted to know what exactly had happened to her son on Iwo Jima. She wrote letters of inquiry, but no one would tell her the truth. Eventually she got an answer, but not through official Marine channels.

Her son, Al, told me that after the war "a man from northern Wisconsin" came to their home in Milwaukee and told Frances that Iggy had died a quick death in battle. My father did not tell her the real story of torture. For one of the few times in his life, I suspect, John Bradley had to choose between compassion and candor. Still, just the visit alone—the reminder of the nightmarish fighting on Iwo Jima—must have been painful for Iggy's mother.

The last two Japanese defenders on Iwo surrendered on January 8, 1949. They emerged from the caves clean and well fed. They decided to give up after reading, in a fragment of the U.S. Army newspaper *Stars and Stripes,* of how American forces were celebrating Christmas in Japan. This told them that the war was over. For four years they had foraged food and clothing in nighttime raids on the compounds of American occupation troops on the island.

The photograph continued to maintain its hold on the American imagination. In early 1949 Republic Studios announced that production was under way on an ambitious motion picture depicting the role of the Marines in the Pacific war. The big-budget epic would star John Wayne and portray Marines training in New Zealand, fighting on Tarawa, on leave in Hawaii, and, in the closing few minutes, landing on Iwo Jima.

To ensure bountiful box office receipts, Republic Studios executives decided to call the movie *Sands of Iwo Jima.* And they wanted the three survivors to raise the flag as the climax to the movie.

Soon, even though little of the movie concerned Iwo Jima, the flag-raising image became central to its marketing. Republic took no chances and asked the help of the Marines in bringing the flag raisers on board. Aware by now of John's reclusiveness and the unpredictability of Ira, the Marines contacted Ira, Rene, and John one at a time, informing each that the other two had agreed to participate. Thus each man was given to understand that if he backed out, he would ruin the entire movie.

The tactic worked on John Bradley, the one most likely to have resisted. By the end of the experience, my father felt exploited. After returning from Hollywood he wrote his old buddy from Easy Company, former corpsman Cliff Langley, that the actual shooting involving him, Rene, and Ira took all of ten minutes and constituted only two minutes of footage in the final cut. "If you think you will see real action like Iwo Jima by seeing the picture I really think you will be sadly disappointed."

John Bradley had it figured right. The movie had nothing to do with Iwo Jima. But as the studio had guessed, reporters followed the flag raisers on and off the set. And indeed the three generated so much copy that, combined with the movie's title and marketing, box office receipts exceeded everyone's expectations.

Ira moved to Chicago, looking for decent work and maybe a new life. He found work as a tool grinder for International Harvester, but while he had a new home, his old habits didn't change. Soon he gave up his job and was piling up an arrest record that was as bad as in Phoenix.

The press was merciless in chronicling his arrests, but not everyone took advantage. There were earnest attempts by citizens and authorities to help Ira, find him work, rescue him from alcohol. But he resisted. Two months later he was back in Phoenix, and the drinking went on. Ira's war would never end.

In December 1953 Cabbage Bradley—John's father—suffered the heart attack that killed him. I was born two months later, in February 1954, in Antigo, and was given Cabbage's name: James Joseph Bradley.

As I grew up, the photograph's grip on the public imagination went undiminished, though it remained largely unknown to me and my siblings. The gigantic work of art it had inspired—the world's tallest bronze statue, the only monument in the nation's capital commemorating World War II—continued to take shape in Washington.

Sculptor Felix de Weldon had worked three years to create the six basic figures. Then he worked three more years to adorn them with uniforms and equipment. When completed, the statue would rise 110 feet from the ground and would weigh more than 100 tons. The six figures would average about 32 feet in height. Their rifles would be 16 feet long. Its cost was $850,000—every penny of it covered by private donations.

As the unveiling date at Arlington National Cemetery neared, November 10, 1954—the shared birthdays of Mike Strank and the U.S. Marine Corps—the three surviving flag raisers were summoned once more into the nation's spotlight. Rene and Pauline came down from New Hampshire. John and Betty Bradley arrived from Antigo. Ira showed up alone.

The governor of Kentucky had proclaimed November 10 "Iwo Jima Day" in that state in honor of Franklin, and Goldie came to the ceremonies in Washington. All the surviving Stranks were there—Pete, John, Mary, Martha, and Vasil. Ed and Belle

Block were reunited for the first time since Harlon's burial at Weslaco, along with children Maurine and Mel. Rene Gagnon Jr. accompanied his parents.

Joe Rosenthal arrived at the unveiling ceremonies with his wife, Lee, and their two small children. He was elated that his photograph was now immortalized in bronze, but he was amazed to learn, as he walked around the statue, that his name had been left off the inscription on the statue. So had the names of the flag raisers. The only name that appeared on the giant edifice was that of the sculptor, Felix de Weldon.

In the nation's memory, the flag raisers' transformation from individuals to anonymous representative figures had begun.

The face of the black granite did, however, contain an inscription. It was a quotation from Admiral Nimitz immediately after the battle, summing up the Marines' collective heroism on the island. The inscription read:

UNCOMMON VALOR WAS A COMMON VIRTUE.

Seven thousand dignitaries swelled the grounds for the unveiling, including President Eisenhower, Vice President Nixon, General H. M. "Howlin' Mad" Smith, and former Marine commandant Vandegrift—who found himself staring directly at Ira Hayes in the front row facing the monument.

At the moment of unveiling, the lanyard was pulled, the protective draping swung free, and the Iwo Jima memorial statue took its place amid the sacred icons of the nation. The survivors and their families sat staring at it, stunned.

"Awesome," was the way my father later described the moment. "The statue was just so huge, so impressive. I could hardly believe it was a reality."

After the ceremony, the three flag raisers prepared to take their leave of one another. Never again would they meet, never again would they serve the photograph.

NINETEEN

Casualties of War

The nicest veterans in Schenectady, I thought, the kindest and funniest ones, the ones who hated the war the most, were the ones who'd really fought.

—Kurt Vonnegut, *Slaughterhouse-Five*

Within ninety days of the statue's dedication, each of the survivors' lives went its separate way. Rene was still looking for ways to capitalize on his fame, my father fulfilled his singular dream of buying a funeral home, and Ira Hayes went back to his lonely existence in Phoenix.

A week before Christmas 1954, Ira was picked up once more for being drunk and disorderly. Someone figured out that it was his fifty-first arrest, dating back to April 1941. A caseworker for the U.S. Indian Service, Pauline Bates Brown, tried to help him during his latest downfall. "His attitude was not bitterness," she remembered years later, "but some hurt that I couldn't sort out."

On the frigid morning of January 24, 1955—one month shy of ten years since he helped raise the flag—Ira walked over to an abandoned hut about three hundred yards from his small living quarters on the Gila River reservation, where he'd sat in on an all-night card game. The other players included Ira's brothers Kenny and Vernon, the brothers Harry and Mark White, and a murky character named Henry Setoyant. The men drank wine as they played. Ira was winning; Henry Setoyant was not pleased by that fact. By the early morning hours everyone was drunk, and Ira was the drunkest of all.

The White brothers were the first to call it a night. Then Vernon and Kenny said, "Let's go home, Ira." But by that time Ira and Henry Setoyant were arguing, clumsily pushing each other. So Vernon and Kenny left.

His brothers never saw Ira alive again.

The circumstances of his death are not totally clear. Henry Setoyant came to the Hayes household the next morning with the news that Ira was dead. Jobe, Nancy, and Kenny raced across the hard, bare ground toward the abandoned hut. They found Ira's body nearby, next to a rusting car.

The coroner ruled it an accidental death due to overexposure in the freezing weather and too much alcohol. Ira Hayes was thirty-two years old.

Two thousand people gathered outside the Cook Presbyterian Church in Sacaton for services on January 25. Five American flags hung at the altar. At 2 P.M. six young Pima Marine reservists bore Ira's coffin into the little church and up the central aisle past two rows of benches to the altar. Ira was dressed in a green Marine uniform. A choir sang hymns in Pima and then in English.

Ira was finally at peace.

The following day his body lay in state at the Arizona Capitol rotunda. Thousands stood in line to pay tribute, overflowing the rotunda and spilling far outside the Capitol. The state legislature stood in recess; Governor Ernest W. McFarland gave the eulogy. Like his friend Mike Strank, Ira was buried at Arlington National Cemetery.

Rene attended the burial. When a reporter asked him about Ira, the old frictions slipped away. "Let's say he had a little dream in his heart that someday the Indian would be like the white man—be able to walk all over the United States."

John did not attend. But from his home in Antigo he remarked that Ira's death "makes him truly a war casualty."

The photograph will forever inspire words about glory and valor among those who see the figures as immortals. To those of us who knew them as ordinary men, there's another side to the story. Imagine six boys from your youth. Line them up in your mind. They are eighteen to twenty-four years old. Select them now; see them. How many marriages, how many children will intersect their lives? Now consider that other than my father, only one other flag raiser married. And that other than my family, the only offspring of the six flag raisers was Rene Gagnon Jr.

In my talks with him, Rene junior confided that his dad considered his participation in the most revered military moment in history to be "as significant as going to the mailbox." I chuckled; it was something my father could have said.

Rene junior described his father's life as almost schizophrenic: a celebrity one minute and a John Doe the next. "It was an emotional roller coaster," Rene junior said. "He would lead a normal life and then he would be invited to a parade, a function, and he would show up and be treated like a little god. . . . It was stop-and-go heroism."

But Rene never stepped away from his roller coaster. Despite all the stress, he didn't seem to want to. Lacking my father's clear focus on avoiding the spotlight, Rene willingly accepted almost every interview, every chance to be in a parade, every opportunity to make a speech that came his way.

Then on October 12, 1979, a janitor discovered that the door to the boiler room of one of his buildings was jammed. He got a crowbar and pried it open. On the floor lay fellow janitor Rene Gagnon, dead. In his hand was the inside handle to the door. Apparently he had dislodged it as he grappled with the door in the throes of his heart attack. He was fifty-four.

Papers across the country ran the story on page one, with "Rene Gagnon" and "Iwo Jima flag" attached in the headlines. Many of the stories noted that the only remaining survivor among the six flag raisers was John Bradley, fifty-six, a funeral director in Antigo, Wisconsin. But "Bradley was in Canada vacationing Saturday and couldn't be reached for comment."

Rene was first interred in a Manchester mausoleum, and then, two years later, at Arlington National Cemetery. On July 7, 1981, newspapers carried photographs of Pauline at the U.S. Marine Corps War Memorial, gazing up at the bronze image of her hero on the day of his Arlington burial. "This is our thirty-sixth wedding anniversary, so the day has special meaning to me," she told the press.

The headstones for Mike and Ira at Arlington are similar to all the others there: simple white slabs that list only their names, ranks, and birth and death dates.

But Pauline saw to it that Rene's stone was distinctive. On its back is a bronze relief of the flag raising and an inscription:

FOR GOD AND HIS COUNTRY
HE RAISED OUR FLAG IN BATTLE
AND SHOWED A MEASURE OF HIS PRIDE
AT A PLACE CALLED IWO JIMA
WHERE COURAGE NEVER DIED

TWENTY

Common Virtue

There are no great men. Just great challenges which ordinary men, out of necessity, are forced by circumstances to meet.

—Admiral William F. "Bull" Halsey

By the early 1980s the men of Easy Company were in their sixties. Their families grown, their work lives nearing an end, many of them felt an urge, long dormant, to reconnect with one another, to remember with their buddies.

Dave Severance became the catalyst for these reconnections. A career Marine, highly decorated, he retired with the rank of colonel in 1968. But as with anyone who had walked in the black sands, Iwo Jima would remain the defining event of his life.

With the instincts of a company captain, Dave compiled a list of Easy Company veterans and sent out invitations. My dad received them all but never went to a single reunion. The burden of being an "immortal hero" and the press attention he'd attract made it impossible.

"I'd love to go," he told my brother Steve once, "but I couldn't just go and be myself and visit with the guys I wanted to. I couldn't just be one of the guys."

Or maybe it was something else. Something too painful to re-open. In 1964, when he was forty and I was nine, my father hinted at why he couldn't talk about Iwo Jima. My third-grade class was studying American history. When we got to World War II, there, on page ninety-eight of our textbook, was the famous photograph. My teacher told the class that my father was a hero. I was proud as only a young son can be.

That afternoon I sat near the back door of our house with my history book open to that page, waiting for Dad to come home from work. When he finally walked through the door, I jumped toward him before he'd even had a chance to take off his coat.

"Dad!" I exclaimed. "Look! There's your picture! My teacher says you're a hero and she wants you to speak to my class. Will you give a speech?"

My father didn't answer me right away. He closed the door and walked me gently over to the kitchen table. He sat down across from me. He took my textbook and looked at the photograph. Then he gently closed the book.

After a moment he said, "I can't talk to your class. I've forgotten everything."

That was often his excuse, that he couldn't remember.

But he went on: "Jim, your teacher said something about heroes. . . ."

I shifted expectantly in my chair, waiting to hear some

stories of valor. Instead he looked me directly in my nine-year-old eyes, signaling that he'd like to embed an idea in my brain for the rest of my life. He said: "I want you to always remember something. The heroes of Iwo Jima are the guys who didn't come back."

More than six years went by before I discussed the subject with him again. And for some reason, on one ordinary night—it was 1970—it all bubbled to the surface.

It was just a normal evening in the Bradley household. Everyone was asleep except for Dad and me. He was forty-six then. I was sixteen and in high school. The two of us, as we often did, were watching the Johnny Carson show. For some reason I brought up the subject that I knew by then was practically taboo: Iwo Jima.

He gave a half smile at me, looked back at the TV—the screen reflecting in his glasses—then shook his head, sighed, and glanced at me again.

I pushed. "Well, Dad, you were there. The battle of Iwo Jima is a historical fact. It happened. You must remember something."

My father broke a long silence.

"I have tried so hard to block this out," he said. "To forget it. We could choose a buddy to go in with. My buddy was a guy from Milwaukee. We were pinned down in one area. Someone elsewhere fell injured and I ran to help out, and when I came back my buddy was gone. I couldn't figure out where he was. I could see all around, but he wasn't there. And nobody knew where he was.

"A few days later someone yelled that they'd found him. They called me over because I was a corpsman. The Japanese had pulled him underground and tortured him. It was terrible. I've tried so hard to forget all this.

"And then I visited his parents after the war and just lied to them. 'He didn't suffer at all,' I told them. 'He didn't feel a thing, didn't know what hit him,' I said. I just lied to them."

Listening to Dad, I didn't know what to say. I was young, unable to fathom the depths of emotion he had just revealed. Today I realize that one reason for his silence on the war no doubt had something to do with Iggy. Maybe his buddy's brutal death was a reminder to John of the ultimate insanity of war, of the worst kind of behavior of one human being to another. Maybe it struck a nerve even deeper than all the tableaux of his helping wounded comrades and withstanding more than a month of desperate battle.

But that night, when he'd finished speaking, we just sat in silence, Dad and I, letting Johnny Carson's next guest change the subject.

My father's heart was in bad shape by Christmas of 1993: open-heart surgery, irregular heartbeat. He was seventy and had mortality on his mind. He wrote his own Christmas cards that year. He reached down through the years and sent them out to his Easy Company buddies. When I met and interviewed those men after his death, they told me that John had sporadically written little Christmas notes over the years. But his 1993 card was downright chatty and included a photograph of his extended family. Had he known it would be his last?

John Bradley's death of a stroke in January 1994 was reported around the world, and we received clippings from as far away as Johannesburg, Hong Kong, and Tokyo. The last surviving flag raiser had died.

To us Bradleys the title "flag raiser" seemed distant and disconnected from the dad that we knew and loved. Fred Berner, editor of the Antigo *Daily Journal*, got it right when he wrote: "John Bradley will be forever memorialized for a few moments' action at the top of a remote Pacific mountain. We prefer to remember him for his life. If the famous flag raising at Iwo Jima symbolizes American patriotism and valor, Bradley's quiet, modest nature and philanthropic efforts shine as an example of the best of small-town American values."

Steve, Tom, Joe, my mother, and I were all by his side in the hospital when he died.

My mother cradled his head, brushed his hair, kissed his forehead. We all touched and kissed him. His breathing got weaker.

"Jack, are you leaving us now?" Betty Van Gorp Bradley whispered. "It's all right if you leave us when you're ready. It's all right, Jack."

At 2:12 A.M. on Tuesday, January 11, 1994, John Bradley took a small breath, exhaled, and died.

The wake for Dad was held in the funeral home where he had comforted so many. It was the largest anyone could remember.

The morning after the wake, just before the church service, we had the closing-of-casket ceremony at the funeral home. This was the family's last chance to say good-bye to husband, father, father-in-law, grandpa.

Some of our family placed small personal items in his casket: a poem, a ring. I walked down the hall of the Bradley Funeral Home and entered my father's office. I faced the only photo hanging there. I gently removed it from the wall and returned to my father's side.

I turned to my family to get their attention. I held the photo high. All could see themselves in it, posed in a family reunion shot that John Bradley had never tired of bragging about.

"That is the only photo he cared about," I said, and then slid it into his casket.

One of my dad's finer qualities was simplicity. The only two songs I ever heard him sing, for example, were "Home on the Range" and "I've Been Working on the Railroad." He lived by simple values, values his children could understand and live by. He had a knack for breaking things down into quiet, basic truths.

"It's as simple as that," he'd say. "Simple as that." And that was how he looked upon that 1/400th of a second on Iwo Jima.

In the saga of the figures in the photograph, my dad came to play a unique role. He was the "last survivor" for fifteen years. And being the only one left, he endured increased demands from authors, journalists, and documentarians. He politely refused them all—until Betty asked. She wanted him to give his first and last taped interview in 1985. "Do it for your grand-children," she implored.

The transcript of this interview has never been published. I obtained it after my dad's death. My father answers the inter-viewer's questions carefully, weighing every word. Asked to de-scribe his participation in the raising of a pole, John Bradley says: "When I came upon the scene, they were just finishing at-taching the flag to the pole and they were just ready to raise it up. I just did what anybody else would have done. I just gave them a hand. That's the way it is in combat. You just help any-one who needs a hand. They didn't ask for my help. I just jumped in and gave them a hand."

John then speaks for all the flag raisers, something he had never done before. He wanted to convey a message that he was sure the other guys would endorse: "People refer to us as heroes. We certainly weren't heroes. And I speak for the rest of the guys as well."

After spending five years researching their lives, the boys cer-tainly seem like heroes to me. I admit it.

But I must defer to my father. He was there. He knew the guys, knew what they did. His hands were on that pole. And John was a straight arrow all his life. He said the same things about the flag raising at sixty-two as he had at twenty-two. And he was confident enough in his conclusion to claim the right to speak for the other guys.

So I will take my dad's word for it: Mike, Harlon, Franklin,

Ira, Rene, and Doc, the men of Easy Company—they just did what anybody would have done, and they were not heroes.

They were boys of common virtue.
Called to duty.
Brothers and sons. Friends and neighbors.
And fathers.
It's as simple as that.

ACKNOWLEDGMENTS

I was ten years old when the war ended.
I thought the returning veterans were giants
who had saved the world from barbarism.
I still think so. I remain a hero worshiper.
Over the decades I've interviewed thousands of
the veterans. It is a privilege to hear their stories,
then write them up.

—Stephen Ambrose

Walking Harlon's football field with his brother Ed . . . listening to Mary Strank describe her last visit with brother Mike . . . standing with Kenny Hayes over the spot where he found Ira dead. How can I thank the flag raisers' relatives who accepted me as family? You gave me five more brothers.

Dad, now I know why you didn't talk about Iwo Jima. And I'm glad I know.

To my family, thank you for trusting me with this story. I tried to honor your trust by getting it right.

Dave Severance guided my search for the flag raisers' pasts. He demonstrated limitless patience for my endless questions, and this book could not have been written without his help. My life has been enriched getting to know this American hero.

Only one man in the world could get my mother to Iwo Jima. I asked that man to help me. "Of course," he replied. Marines are special people. And Charles Krulak is a special Marine.

Katie Hall of Bantam Books took a risk by acquiring the original edition of this book, and edited it with professional and loving care. Her contribution will remain invisible to the reader, but I know and will always appreciate her superb efforts.

My agent, Jim Hornfischer, bravely took me on after I had managed to accumulate twenty-seven publishers' rejections. It was Jim's idea to team me with Ron Powers, whose reputation for quality was key to making this project a reality. Thanks, Jim and Ron!

To my many friends and supporters whose encouragement was never-ending—I wish I could add another chapter and list your names.

I have lived and worked in Japan and have warm friendships with a number of Japanese. Nothing I have written detracts from the deep respect I have for Japan and her people.

Easy Company member Jesse Boatwright made a remark to me once that reflects the sentiments of almost all the Marines and corpsmen who contributed to this book: "You might think we did something special there on Iwo, but we were just ordinary guys doing our duty."

To Mr. Boatwright and his comrades, yes, I understand your feeling that you were just doing your duty. And I hope you can appreciate the profound admiration I have for you and your

actions out in the Pacific. You ordinary guys, you heroes of
Iwo Jima.

James Bradley
January 2000
Rye, New York

PHOTO CREDITS

Jack Bradley and family (from the collection of Elizabeth Bradley)

Rene Gagnon (from the collection of Rene Gagnon Jr.)

Ira Hayes and father (from the collection of Sara Bernal)

Franklin Sousley with dog (from the collection of Geneva Price)

Mike Strank, First Communion (from the collection of Mary Strank Pero)

Harlon Block and brothers (© Edward F. Block Jr.)

Harlon Block, Marine (from the collection of Catherine Pierce Foster)

Rene Gagnon, Marine (from the collection of the Wright Museum)

Jack Bradley, Navy (from the collection of Elizabeth Bradley)

Franklin Sousley, Marine (from the collection of Geneva Price)

Mike Strank in camouflage (from the collection of Mary Strank Pero)

Ira Hayes, paratrooper (© National Archives)

Iwo Jima, 1945 (photo by E. W. "Bill" Peck, from the collection of Carol
   Peck Sanders)

D day—to the beaches (© National Archives)

First flag lowered, second raised (© National Archives; Louis Lowery, USMC
   photographer)

Rosenthal photo, horizontal (© AP/Wide World Photos)

The New York Times (© *The New York Times*)

Felix de Weldon sculpts Rene Gagnon (from the collection of Elizabeth Bradley)

USMC Memorial (© James Bradley)

James Bradley and family atop Suribachi (© Joseph Bradley)

BIBLIOGRAPHY

Alexander, Joseph H. *Storm Landings: Epic Amphibious Battles in the Central Pacific.* Annapolis, MD: Naval Institute Press, 1997.

Bartley, Whitman. *Iwo Jima: Amphibious Epic, A Marine Corps Monograph.* Nashville, TN: The Battery Press, 1988.

Bergerud, Eric. *Touched with Fire: The Land War in the South Pacific.* New York: Penguin Books, 1997.

Chang, Iris. *The Rape of Nanking: The Forgotten Holocaust of World War II.* New York: Basic Books, 1997.

Chapin, John C., Cpt., USMC. *Top of the Ladder.* Marines in WWII Commemorative Series. Washington, DC: Marine Corps Historical Center.

Conner, Howard. *The Spearhead.* Nashville, TN: The Battery Press, 1987.

Dobyns, Henry, and Frank W. Porter III, gen. ed. *The Pima Maricopa.* New York: Chelsea House Publishers, 1989.

Hemingway, Albert. *Ira Hayes: Pima Marine.* Lanham, MD: University Press of America, 1988.

Ienaga, Saburo. *The Pacific War: A Critical Perspective on Japan's Role in World War II.* New York: Random House, 1978.

Linderman, Gerald F. *The World Within War: America's Combat Experience in World War II.* Cambridge, MA: Harvard University Press, 1999.

Monks, John A., Jr. *A Ribbon and a Star: The Third Marines at Bougainville.* New York: Holt and Co., 1945.

Newcomb, Richard. *Iwo Jima.* New York: Bantam Books, 1995.

Ricks, Thomas E. *Making the Corps.* New York: Scribner, 1997.

Ross, Bill D. *Iwo Jima—Legacy of Valor.* New York: The Vanguard Press, 1985.

Shay, Jonathan. *Achilles in Vietnam: Combat Trauma and the Undoing of Character.* New York: Touchstone Books, 1995.

Sherrod, Robert. *Tarawa: The Story of a Battle.* Fredericksburg, TX: Admiral Nimitz Foundation, 1986.

Sledge, E. B. *With the Old Breed: At Peleliu and Okinawa.* New York: Oxford University Press, 1981.

Smith, Holland M., and Percy Finch. *Coral and Brass.* Nashville, TN: The Battery Press, 1989.

Tatum, Charles W. *Iwo Jima: Red Blood, Black Sand: Pacific Apocalypse.* Stockton, CA: Charles W. Tatum Publishing, 1995.

Thomey, Tedd. *Immortal Images: A Personal History of Two Photographers and the Flag Raising on Iwo Jima.* Annapolis, MD: Naval Institute Press, 1996.

Tibbets, Paul W. *Flight of the Enola Gay.* Columbus, OH: Mid-Coast Marketing, 1989.

Vedder, James S. *Combat Surgeon: Up Front with the 27th Marines.* Novato, CA: Presidio Press, 1984.

Wheeler, Richard. *The Bloody Battle for Suribachi.* Annapolis, MD: Naval Institute Press, 1994.

———. *Iwo.* Annapolis, MD: Naval Institute Press, 1994.

INDEX

ABOUT THE AUTHORS

James Bradley is the son of John "Doc" Bradley, one of the six flag raisers. Raised in Wisconsin, he studied at the University of Notre Dame and Sophia University in Tokyo and graduated with a degree in East Asian history from the University of Wisconsin. In the course of writing *Flags of Our Fathers*, James Bradley conducted more than three hundred interviews with World War II veterans and their families. He lives in Rye, New York, and welcomes visitors at www.jamesbradley.com.

Ron Powers is a Pulitzer prize–winning journalist and the author of *Dangerous Water: A Biography of the Boy Who Became Mark Twain*. He lives in Vermont.

Michael French has several books for young readers to his credit, including *Basher Five-Two: The True Story of F-16 Fighter Pilot Captain Scott O'Grady*, which he co-wrote with Scott O'Grady. Michael French makes his home in New Mexico.